The book you hold in your hands is not a complete biography or a total philosophy of the Wu-Tang Clan. Instead, it represents an introduction to some of the basic principles of Wu-Tang thought and artistry, a glimpse into some of the ideas and life events that shaped the Clan. Consider it an accompaniment to the album *Enter the Wu-Tang: 36 Chambers*—every important aspect of the foundation is touched on here, including spirituality, kung fu, chess, and so forth—but to the true student this is only a doorway to a fuller understanding. Sample the knowledge, wisdom, and understanding by dropping into separate tracks, or read the book straight through; this is a path, not the destination. For those who seek, the 36th chamber still awaits. Let the saga begin.

THE RZA
December, 2004

THE

WU-TANG

MANUAL

PHOTOGRAPHS BY

CRAIG WETHERBY

MICHAEL LAVINE

SOPHIA CHANG

FRANK 151

RIVERHEAD FREESTYLE
NEW YORK

THE

WU-TANG

MANUAL

THE RZA

WITH CHRIS NORRIS

The Berkley Publishing Group
Published by the Penguin Group
Penguin Group (USA) Inc.
375 Hudson Street, New York, New York 10014, USA
Penguin Group (Canada), 10 Alcorn Avenue, Toronto, Ontario M4V 3B2, Canada (a division of Pearson Penguin Canada Inc.)
Penguin Books Ltd., 80 Strand, London WC2R 0RL, England
Penguin Group Ireland, 25 St. Stephen's Green, Dublin 2, Ireland (a division of Penguin Books Ltd.)
Penguin Group (Australia), 250 Camberwell Road, Camberwell, Victoria 3124, Australia (a division of Pearson Australia Group Pty. Ltd.)
Penguin Books India Pvt. Ltd., 11 Community Centre, Panchsheel Park, New Delhi—110 017, India
Penguin Group (NZ), cnr Airborne and Rosedale Roads, Albany, Auckland 1310, New Zealand (a division of Pearson New Zealand Ltd.)
Penguin Books (South Africa) (Pty.) Ltd., 24 Sturdee Avenue, Rosebank, Johannesburg 2196, South Africa

Penguin Books Ltd., Registered Offices: 80 Strand, London WC2R 0RL, England

THE WU-TANG MANUAL

PRINTING HISTORY
First Riverhead Freestyle trade paperback edition: January 2005
Riverhead Freestyle trade paperback ISBN: 978-1-59448-018-8

This book has been catalogued with the Library of Congress.

PRINTED IN THE UNITED STATES OF AMERICA

20 19 18 17 16 15 14 13

THE

WU-TANG

MANUAL

contents

.

BOOK

ONE

RZA

And the RZA, he the sharpest motherfucker in the whole clan, he always on point. Razor sharp—with the beats, with the rhymes, whatever . . .

AKA

The Abbot, Bobby Digital, Bobby Steels, Prince Rakeem, the RZA-recta, the Scientist, Prince Delight, Prince Dynamite, Ruler Zig-Zag-Zig Allah

BIRTH NAME

Robert F. Diggs, named after the second Kennedy brother, Robert F. Kennedy

DROPPED

July 5, 1969

PROVINCE

Brownsville, Brooklyn, official Shaolin resident at age fourteen; original group, All in Together Now, with GZA and ODB.

Organizer, producer, and mastermind of the Wu-Tang Clan. Creator of one of the most influential sounds and styles in hip-hop history. Favors scientific rhyme attack and verbal chi gong.

JOINTS

Ooh We Love You Rakeem EP (1991); *RZA as Bobby Digital in Stereo* (1998); *RZA as Bobby Digital: Digital Bullet* (2001); *The World According to RZA* (2003); *Birth of a Prince* (2003)

THE LEGEND OF RZA

Wu-Tang niggas are famous for having lots of names, lots of pseudonyms and alter-egos. It's been like that from the beginning. I personally have gone as Prince Dynamite, Prince Rap Delight, the Rap Scientist—we used to do that all day, think up rap names. Dirty and I had at least ten names apiece—for a while, *he* was Prince Delight and *I* was Prince Dynamite. But before long, the names started to become real.

When I did my first record, I was Prince Rakeem, and I had a song called "Pza Pza Pumping." That song was big in my neighborhood, but niggas used to call me *Rza Rza* Rakeem because I wrote "Razor" as a graffiti tag. Niggas would say, "Rza Rza Rakeem—you razor sharp still." So the sound was already in my head, floating around, ready to take form.

Then, my teacher in Islam had us removing the S's. He was saying, "We don't need no S anymore. We're completing ourselves with a Z." In Divine Mathematics, the Z stands for Zig-Zag-Zig, which means knowledge, wisdom, and understanding—the last letter of the alphabet and the final step of consciousness. So finally, I just thought of the name as letters, not a word. R Z A. It stands for Ruler–Knowledge-Wisdom-and-Understanding–Allah.

These names reflected changes I was going through. There was a war going on inside me then. Back in the '80s, I lost it. I became a problem for the world. I wasn't living righteous. And, in one moment of clarity, I saw that. I looked to GZA, who was my teacher in Islam, and I said, "Yo, you're doing the same thing"–because he was down with me in the negativity. And we changed, both of us. We had no choice. It was either that, go crazy, or go starving.

So today, one of the names people still call me is the Resurrector–like I bring people back to life. In a way, the first one that I resurrected was me.

GZA

And the GZA, the Genius is just the Genius. He's the backbone of the whole joint. He the head, let's put it that way. We form like Voltron and the GZA happen to be the head.

AKA
Genius, Justice, Allah Justice, Maximillion, the Scientist, the Head

BIRTH NAME
Gary Grice

DROPPED
August 22, 1966

PROVINCE
Bedford-Stuyvesant, Brooklyn

STYLE AND PROFILE
Cousin of RZA and ODB, founding member of the Wu-Tang, and first Wu MC to record an album, *Words from the Genius*, out a few years

before the Clan's debut. Known for the invincible dopeness of his rhyme style.

JOINTS

Words from the Genius (1991); *Liquid Swords* (1995); *Beneath the Surface* (1999); *Legend of the Liquid Sword* (2002)

The Legend of GZA

There's something about GZA, something about the way he talks that makes niggas tremble.

One day me and a few of my brothers were pinned down inside an apartment building. Some guys from the projects had beef with us and we were trapped in there by maybe eight guys. GZA, he was the first one who had knowledge of himself, but he also had this kind of naturally dominant vibe to him. So he puts on this Muslim crown—a kind of skullcap with a tassle—and puts on his star, and walks out there alone. He strides out and he says, "I'm Allah Justice, boy! From Brooklyn!"

And everybody submitted to him! They saw him, heard him, and they knew they didn't want problems with him. You didn't want problems with the gods back then. But GZA, he had this extra power in his presence.

Justice is his righteous name. The full name is Allah Justice. That's why you look on the cover of "Protect Ya Neck" single, it's spelled J-I-Z-Z-A. His name back in the day was Gangsta G. He was Gangsta G and Dirty was the Genius. Then Dirty became the Professor for a while, and we traded off. Finally, it was clear who the Genius was.

Rakim, Kool G Rap, Kane—I've listened to them since day one. I've met them, and they're exceptional MCs. I mean, *exceptional* MCs. But to my personal taste, none of them could touch the GZA. I knew it in my heart way back before the Wu-Tang, and I strived to be like him, not like them. GZA's the only one with a style that actually instilled fear in me.

On his first album, there was this one rhyme: "I met a young brother/How young/About eight/Smooth, intelligent/And rather quite straight/So I greeted him/And struck a conversation/To see if this youngster had some self-motivation . . ." It's simple, but it's intentionally simple. It's slow, deliberate, and fierce. This was back when niggas were using all kinds of big words and trying to rap fast and fill the space up with syllables. But GZA was taking it down to something else. You caught real drama off his rhymes and his style. He could make "cat" and "rat" sound *threatening.*

OL' DIRTY BASTARD

. . . And then we got the Old Dirty Bastard, 'cause there ain't no father to his style. That's why he the Old Dirty Bastard.

AKA

Dirty, the Professor, the Bebop Specialist, the Specialist, Prince Delight, Ason Unique, Unique Ason, Osiris, Cyrus, Big Baby Jesus, Dirt McGirt, Dirt Schultz, Ol' Dirt Dawg, Joe Bananas, Freeloading Rusty

BIRTH NAME

Russell Jones

DROPPED

November 15, 1968

PROVINCE

Linden Plaza, East New York, Brooklyn Zoo

STYLE AND PROFILE

Cousin of RZA and GZA, member of the rap group D.R.U.G., freelance rhyme terrorist. The most wild, unorthodox mic style in the Wu-Tang Clan—and possibly hip-hop history. Also has longest and most flavorful arrest sheet.

JOINTS

Return to the 36 Chambers: The Dirty Version (1995); *O.D.B.E.P.* (1996); *Nigga Please* (1999); *The Dirty Story: The Best of O.D.B.* (2001); *The Trials and Tribulations of Russell Jones* (2002)

THE LEGEND OF ODB

In every kung-fu movie, there's always the dirty bastard, the dirty rat; somebody who, no matter what he does, does wrong. Even when he does right, his *intent* is to do wrong. Well, that's Dirty in real life.

He'd rather do it to a girl that *got* a guy than a girl without a guy. I've seen him bring a girl and her boyfriend to the hotel—and they're hanging with him. Then he'll take the guy to our room and say, "Hey, meet the RZA," and then he'll go off with the girl. That's Dirty. It's like he can't help it.

He was always first to get into something since we were little kids. One day, we were about sixteen, and some guys rolled up on him and a couple of the other cousins in Brooklyn with a shotgun. And ODB just took the gun right out of the guy's hand. The motherfucker snatched the gun and turned it back on him. You've heard all the stories since then, but that's the one I always remember. No one else did shit like that—not and live to tell.

He's a true American free spirit. He scares some people, but other people just love him because he'll do what they wish they would do but are scared. At the same time, I don't think any rapper in hip-hop expresses as much soul as ODB. In his lyrics and his style, ODB has soul, funk, melody, and something outside the realm of what you can name.

There's only one Dirty. The planet couldn't handle another.

METHOD MAN

Then it's the Method Man—it's like mad different methods to the way I do my shit. Basically, Method Man is like "Roll that shit, light that shit, smoke it." Nah-mean?

AKA
The Panty Raider, Methtical, Tical, Ticallion Stallion, Hott Nikkels, Hot Nixon, Iron Lung, John-John McLane, Johnny Blaze, John-John Blaizini, Johnny Dangerous, Shakwon, Ghost Rider, the MZA, Long John Silver

BIRTH NAME
Clifford Smith

DROPPED
April 1, 1971

PROVINCE
Shaolin by way of Hempstead, Long Island

First breakout star of the Wu-Tang Clan. Solo career jump-started by self-titled single on the Wu debut. Star of the suburban TV sitcom *Method and Red*, with Redman. Known for supreme versatility in battle—a rap chameleon, able to switch up every bar.

JOINTS

Tical (1994); *Tical* (2000): *Judgement Day* (1998); *Tical: The Alter Ego Remixes* (1998); *Blackout* (1999); *How High* (Soundtrack) (2001); *Tical 0: The Prequel* (2004)

THE LEGEND OF METHOD MAN

At first, Meth was a guy I took off Staten Island. I probably met him when he was fourteen and I was sixteen. I took him to parties and things he wasn't familiar with. Me and Meth, we'd go to Brooklyn, go to Manhattan, go all over the place. By cab or ferryboat—just go. That's how our life was then.

The main thing I remember about Meth from back in the day: This motherfucker smoked some *weed*. That's why I named him Method Man after Method, or Methtical—the slang we had for weed—because I had never seen anybody smoke as much weed as this nigga.

He had other names, like Panty Raider, which was the name of a neighborhood hit he had. People would call you after your song. It's funny because he was always the heartthrob of the Wu, but he hated that, even back in the day. Every MC is into girls; he just got tagged Panty Raider early on.

He has more flows than any other MC I've ever met. He has more styles, more ways of flowing over the beat than just about anyone. Even on that first joint, "Method Man," you hear him change it up almost every other line. He's just got mad grace. He was always like a Michael Jackson dancing nigga back in the day. And when he's on the mic, it still sounds like dancing.

RAEKWON

Raekwon . . . he the Chef, he cookin' up some marvelous shit, to get your mouth waterin' on some "Oh shit!"

AKA

Lex Diamonds, Louis Diamonds, Rick Diamonds, Shallah

BIRTH NAME

Corey Woods

DROPPED

January 12, 1970

PROVINCE

Shaolin by way of Brooklyn, New York

STYLE AND PROFILE

The most fashion-forward member of the Wu-Tang Clan. Single-handedly ignited the Old-School Mafioso renaissance of mid-to-late

'90s rap with his debut *Only Built 4 Cuban Linx.* Asked everyone on the album to take a new nickname, in honor of the Wu Gambinos crime-family offshoot. Known for the freshest slang in the entire Wu-Tang family.

JOINTS

Only Built 4 Cuban Linx (1995); *Immobilarity* (1999); *The Lex Diamond Story* (2003).

THE LEGEND OF RAEKWON

Rae ... He's got too many stories. He was into so much shit, and most of it I can't really write about here. He was one of the first who really took it from street experience. Raekwon and Ghost are both master criminologists. They're from two different projects, and they really do know how the street trade works. When you hear them rap about it, it's a little more sinister.

A lot of people want to know why Rae is called the Chef. You see him on the inside cover of *Only Built 4 Cuban Linx,* he's at the kitchen sink, with the Pyrex, looking like he's about to cook something up. But at the same time, Rae literally was a chef. He was known for cooking up some really good fish. Whiteys, that's what we ate in the hood, and he could fry up some delicious whiteys. But also, in a bunch of the original Wu-Tang movies, one of the best fighters was this character the Chef. The guy who played him was Yuen Siu Tien, who's the father of Yuen Wo Ping, the action director who choreographed the fight scenes in *The Matrix* and *Kill Bill.* And that Chef, Yuen Siu Tien, he had a pudgy look about him, like Raekwon. So that's another reason we called him the Chef.

The last and maybe most important reason Raekwon is the Chef is his flavor. Since way, way back in the day, he always kept himself fresh. He had the Gumby haircut, the Gucci shoes, and he had the freshest slang of anybody. Slang was his masterpiece, and when Raekwon first got on the mic you'd never heard anybody like that in the whole history of hip-hop. Most people agree the *Cuban Linx* album has the most slang ever in hip-hop. He had his own terms for everything. You know how people would call Q-Tip the Abstract Poet? To me, Raekwon was the ultimate abstract poet. And he was a street hustler, for real. That's a very, very ill combination.

GHOSTFACE KILLAH

Ghostface Killah, knowumsayin', he on some now you see me now you don't.

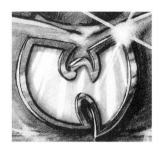

AKA

Iron Man, Tony Starks, Sun God, Wally Champ, Tony Starks, General Tony Starks, Starkey Love, Pretty Toney

BIRTH NAME

Dennis Coles

DROPPED

May 9, 1970

PROVINCE

Stapleton Projects, Shaolin

STYLE AND PROFILE

First swordsman heard on the Wu-Tang debut and the last one to be seen. He appeared in all early Wu-Tang Clan videos wearing a white ski mask. Known for ferocious mic technique, emotional dramatics, and some of the most bizarre, impenetrable language of all Wu-Tang MCs.

JOINTS

Ironman (1996); *Supreme Clientele* (2000); *Bulletproof Wallets* (2001); *Shaolin's Finest* (2003); *The Pretty Toney Album* (2004)

THE MYSTERY OF THE WALLABEE

The Wallabee shoe, manufactured by Clarks, was preferred New York ghetto footwear from the early to late '80s. Ghostface Killah brought them to a new level of excellence.

He was the first person to dye them in two or even three different colors on one shoe. He'd take them all the way to Manhattan, on Canal Street, to have a guy do it for him. He'd bring them back to the hood and nobody had ever seen them before. Wallabees had been around forever but they faded out. And Ghostface came back with them when hip-hop had forgot about them. One thing Wu-Tang did was we brought back a lot of things that hip-hop had forgot: Ballys, Wallabees, the Gucci suits and all that. We brought back the '86, '87 style that was missing.

THE LEGEND OF GHOSTFACE KILLAH

In the kung-fu film *The Mystery of Chess Boxing,* the Ghostface Killer was a villain. But he was the best, best bad guy ever. You walked away from that film knowing his name. When he killed someone, he'd leave behind a little metal plate with a ghost's face on it. And he'd never give up. He might chase you for ten years, but eventually, he'd get you.

But Ghostface is also Iron Man, and always has been. That's because he was known as being very strong in the streets.

I remember a concert at the Harlem Armory in uptown Manhattan. The knights of the Wu were there to perform with other rap crews when a fight broke out. People were fighting onstage, backstage, everywhere. It was just one of those days, when the whole place is fighting. People are swinging and kicking. Coca-Cola cans are flying fast as bullets, hitting people in the head. It was chaos. In the center of it, you see one man.

There he is. Pants down to his knees. Two guys on one arm. Two guys on another arm. Two guys on his legs. He's throwing arms, pushing through—he's just unstoppable. Ghostface. He was like the Thing. Just *throwing* niggas! Ghostface is super strong. He was back then and he still is.

INSPECTAH DECK

Inspectah Deck he's like that dude that'll sit back and watch you play yourself and all that, right? And see you sit there, and know you lying, and he'll take you to court after that—'cause he the Inspector.

AKA

Rebel INS, Rollie Fingers, Fifth Brother, Ayatollah, Manifesto, Charliehorse

BIRTH NAME

Jason Hunter

DROPPED

July 6, 1970

PROVINCE

Park Hill Projects, Shaolin, New York

STYLE AND PROFILE

Primarily an MC, who also produces beats for many Clan affiliates. Often considered the group's unsung hero, kicked off the legendary single "Protect Ya Neck." Known for sharp observation skills, detailed storytelling, and vicious first-verse kickoffs.

JOINTS

Uncontrolled Substance (1999); *The Movement* (2003)

THE LEGEND OF INSPECTAH DECK

Deck was always the cool kid on the block. He's the person that you never see but he's always there, that guy who lurks in the shadows. Even if you didn't think he was there when it went down, he'd seen it. He might have seen you pick your nose when no one else did in the whole party. He was the eyes of the streets. So he was the Inspector—that originally came from Inspector Clouseau, the detective from *The Pink Panther*. And he was the Rebel INS, because that was his tag for writing graffiti.

When we first got into Wu-Tang, Deck had just come back from jail, with some lyrics and some styles. In fact, he reminded me of myself a lot in his choice of lyrics and word patterns. Plus, he lived in a building where a lot of things happened. It was 160 in Park Hill. You hear a lot of Wu-Tang songs that talk about 160—the One-Six-Oh.

One-sixty was the best weed spot and people from all over Staten Island came to it. There was about thirty thousand blacks on Staten Island at that time and, believe me, if you smoked weed, you went to

160. We hung out in front of 160, a lot of people did business there, a lot of people got shot there. But Deck—he *lived* there.

He's also one of the most lyrical swordsmen of all. I like to call him the set-off man because he always sets it off right. He lights the wick that leads to the bomb and once that wick is lit there's no turning back. Listen to the song "C.R.E.A.M."—I know Raekwon gets a lot of credit for that record, but Deck had the most compelling lines: "You got corrupt cops and stage shots and stage blocks." He was saying things that only a news reporter would have said. You could see and feel the reality in his verse.

U-GOD

And then Baby Huey—he a psychopathic thinker . . .

AKA

Golden Arms, Lucky Hands, Universal God of Law, Baby U, Baby Huey, Four-Bar Killer, Ugodz-Illa

BIRTH NAME

Lamont Hawkins

DROPPED

October 11, 1970

PROVINCE

Park Hill Projects, Shaolin, New York

Missing for most of the making of *Enter the Wu-Tang Clan: 36 Chambers*, but returned from jail just in time to get on two tracks. Known for booming voice, compressed rhymes, tight lyrics, and beat-box skills. And temper.

JOINTS

Golden Arms Redemption (1999); *Ugodz-Illa Presents Hillside Scramblers* (2004)

THE LEGEND OF U-GOD

U-God, he's the bass of the group. He's just got that dope-ass low voice. And he's also known as the Four-Bar Killer because he can kill it in four bars. He hits you like in a kung-fu movie, when one motherfucker hits you with a punch from one inch away and it pushes you across the street. U-God can do that.

His name U-God comes from his righteous name, Universal God Allah, which is too long for rap so he switched it up. He's also known as Golden Arms after this villain in kung-fu movies who wore golden bangles that would protect him against all weapons and could kill or maim on their own.

One funny thing about U-God is he was always a lucky motherfucker. For example, he always seemed to come across money. One time, around '86 or '87, he came across a bag with *a lot* of money in it. I don't know where he found it. And then he did it again that year—*twice* in one year. Suddenly he's coming back with cables, a car, Gucci gear. This motherfucker was bad after that.

He was always lucky like that. When there was a drought on something—he got it. So part of his name, to me, is from asking him, "You got that? U got it? U-got?" And U-God always did.

MASTA KILLA

AKA
Noodles High Chief, Jamel Irief

BIRTH NAME
Elgin Turner

DROPPED
August 18, 1969

PROVINCE
East New York, Brooklyn

STYLE AND PROFILE
The Wu-Tang general who keeps the lowest profile. Originally considered the honorary ninth member and last of the original nine to join. Now carrying the torch of the original Wu-Tang family with a solo album, *No Said Date*. An old-school true believer and serious verbal assassin.

JOINTS
No Said Date (2004)

The Legend of Masta Killa

You know you're real if you get to be called Master Killer—that's a very coveted name to martial arts film fans. And Killa, he's a very, very serious brother. He got to be Masta Killa partly because of the way he rocked a baldhead, like the original Master Killer, but mostly because of his skill.

Master Killer was Gordon Liu's character in the original *The Thirty-sixth Chamber* (also called *Master Killer* in the U.S.). He's the young Shaolin monk who trained on each successive level until he attained the thirty-sixth chamber of invincible martial artistry.

In a lot of ways Masta Killa really is like that character because he's like the ultimate Shaolin student. He was never an MC before he came into the Clan. But he came, he studied, he hung out with us all, and he was the original disciple who was brought into the fold. He kept it real throughout, and he's among the most real now. That's why at the beginning of the album *No Said Date,* you hear that kung-fu sample from *Five Deadly Venoms,* about these cats going out to collect the other monks who went wrong.

There's another side of him, too, the street side. That's why he also goes by Noodles, after the Robert De Niro character in the mobster epic *Once Upon a Time in America.* Masta Killa, he's seen some shit. But he wouldn't be Wu-Tang if he hadn't.

BOOK

TWO

HOLY BIBLE

The Qur'an
Text, Translation
and
Commentary
by
Abdullah Yusuf Ali

Sri Aurobindo
Essays on the Gita

HOMER
THE ILIAD
Winner of The Academy of American Poets 1991 London Translation Award
TRANSLATED BY
ROBERT FAGLES
INTRODUCTION AND NOTES BY BERNARD KNOX

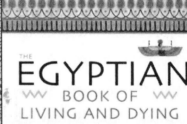THE
EGYPTIAN
BOOK OF
LIVING AND DYING
THE ILLUSTRATED GUIDE TO
ANCIENT EGYPTIAN WISDOM
JOANN FLETCHER

Paulo Coelho
The Illustrated
ALCHEMIST
A FABLE ABOUT FOLLOWING YOUR DREAM
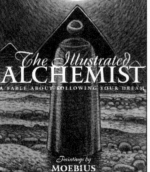Paintings by
MOEBIUS

SHAMBHALA POCKET CLASSICS
THE ART
OF PEACE
Morihei Ueshiba
TRANSLATED BY JOHN STEVENS

THE ART
兵法 OF WAR
SUN TZU
Lionel Giles' classic translation
with
Introduction and Critical Notes
THE OLDEST MILITARY TREATISE IN THE WORLD

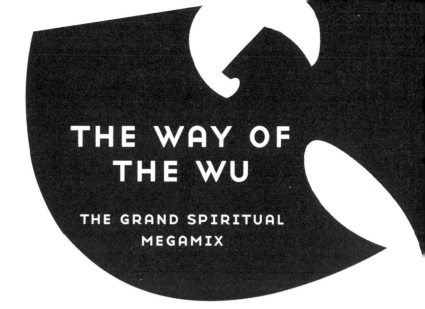

THE WAY OF THE WU

THE GRAND SPIRITUAL MEGAMIX

Believe nothing, no matter where you read it, or who said it, no matter if I have said it, unless it agrees with your own reason and your own common sense.

—THE BUDDHA

THE BIBLE

Everyone's always talking about keeping it real. A lot of times, though, the purest reality comes from something presented as fiction. Some old myths and old stories have reality inside them. They drop deep truth you can't get in a news report or a history book.

For me, the Bible was the first thing that got me interested in finding the real truth in stories. When I was little, I spent a few years down South, where I was raised Baptist. I went to church, learned about Jesus. But when I got to be about seven, I moved back to Brooklyn, and my mother gave me a kids' version of Bible stories. I must have read that over fifty times. It sparked something in me.

Samson

The Old Testament is where all the magic happens. Joseph, Moses, Noah—they're all magical stories. But it's also about murders, wars, violence—it's real. They're all real stories about a couple of mighty niggas against a lot of odds.

Right away, I was sucked in. Solomon, how he's going to cut the baby in half to solve a dispute? Samson, how his hair was the source of his strength? When I read about Samson, I wanted braids because I felt I had something in common with him. As a man, I realize it wasn't really his hair; it was what it represented. It was his true self.

As I get older, I read the Bible and I get something different out of it each time. I read it now and I think about cities that were destroyed by falling rocks, like Sodom and Gomorrah. That's a funny story. They were so fucked up that shit had to fall from the sky on these niggas. You could say a spirit did it, or they did it to themselves. I don't care if you don't believe in God, you know that mob power exists and you know the way you live attracts certain forces to you. They attracted their own destruction. Nowadays, you don't have to look hard to see that that happens for real.

GRECO-ROMAN MYTHOLOGY

The Bible teaches that Greek mythology is wrong, but to me it's all literature. They've all got similar stories, they're just different ways of looking at the same thing. From the beginning, I was attracted to both the reality *and* the fantasy in them.

As a child, I soaked up all kinds of historical tales. I'm a reader, so I just soaked up everything. I read the *Iliad*, the *Odyssey*—I read school versions for kids—and I got deep into the story of Perseus. He was a son of Zeus, a hero that went and cut off the head of Medusa. I felt the fantasy part, the whole power of something beyond what I knew. It was deep to me.

SUPREME MATHEMATICS – THE NATION OF GODS AND EARTHS

They don't know who the true living God is nor their origins in the world so they worship what they know not.

—POPA WU

When a king tried to marry the beautiful Danae against her will, her son Perseus, whose father was Zeus, asked the price for his mother's freedom. The king demanded the impossible: Perseus must bring back the head of the serpent-haired monster Medusa, whose gaze turned men to stone. Perseus set off and, through cunning, heroism, and the help of certain gods, succeeded. He beheaded Medusa with a sword made of adamant—a hard, black, legendary stone capable of slicing through anything.

In 1981, when I was eleven, the same year Grandmaster Flash's *Adventures on the Wheels of Steel* came out, GZA began teaching me about two things: MCing and Supreme Mathematics.

GZA was the first one that I heard talk about God inside, instead of looking up into the sky for God. That snapped a revelation inside my head.

That was the first time I heard something that made sense externally and internally. Being in poverty and one of the oppressed people in America, you know you're limited, but you feel like you shouldn't be. These teachers taught us, You are the original man of all civilization. Hearing that when you're a kid, you're like, "Whoa. Who, me?" It was power. But you grow to understand that this knowledge is not just for black or white. It's stuff the whole human race needs to know.

The original Wu-Tang logo, designed in 1991 by Mathematics

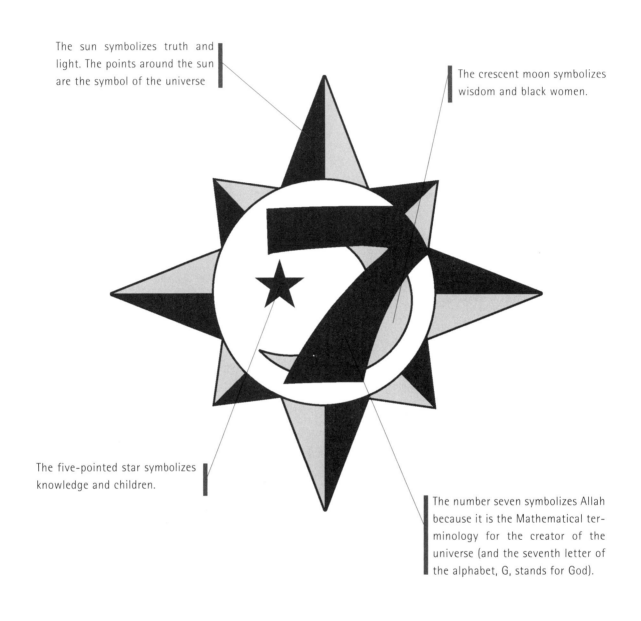

The sun symbolizes truth and light. The points around the sun are the symbol of the universe

The crescent moon symbolizes wisdom and black women.

The five-pointed star symbolizes knowledge and children.

The number seven symbolizes Allah because it is the Mathematical terminology for the creator of the universe (and the seventh letter of the alphabet, G, stands for God).

The first thing you have to do is to memorize 120 questions and answers. The first question is "Who is the original man?" And the answer is, "The original man is the Asiatic Black man, the Maker, the Owner, the Cream of the planet Earth, the Father of Civilization, and God of the Universe." GZA was my teacher and he tested me. I went through the whole thing with him. Even the words "the" and "a" had to be in the right places back then. By the end of '82, when I was twelve, I knew the whole 120.

You can get tested on these questions and answers at any given moment by any person. In the old days, you could walk to the corner and there'd be two brothers there who knew it, too, and they'd feel it was their duty to test you.

A cipher was held by the brothers standing in a circle testing you—you had to show and prove. The word "cipher" in hip-hop comes from that. So does slang like "dropping science," "break it down," and even the expression "word." That's what you say when someone expresses a deep truth: Word. Even the greeting "Peace" come from Islam.

About 80 percent of hip-hop comes from the Five Percent. These same brothers are the fathers of a lot of our MC styles. Rakim, Big Daddy Kane, Poor Righteous Teachers, Busta Rhymes, Leaders of the New School, Guru from Gangstarr, Pete Rock and CL Smooth, Mobb Deep, Kam, Professor Griff, Paris, Jeru the Damaja—in a lot of ways, hip-hop *is* the Five Percent.

In 1964, Clarence 13X—a student minister at the Nation of Islam's Temple Number Seven in Harlem—opened his own street academy. He took the name Allah, or the Father, and started teaching a condensed version of the Nation's *Lost-Found Lessons*. Like the Nation, the Father's school refuted most accepted history and organized religion, denying the existence of any supernatural "mystery god," and substituting the idea that the black man himself is god—a god of his own family, universe, and destiny.

This was the foundation of the Five Percent Nation, whose name comes from the belief that its followers are the 5 percent of humanity who live a righteous life and manifest the black man's true divine nature. Eighty-five percent are the mentally deaf and blind, while the remaining 10 percent are devils who have knowledge but intentionally keep the rest ignorant.

The father felt that endangered poor black youth required a faster approach to the teachings than the one the Nation was offering and so he broke the lessons down to their core, what followers call "the 120"—120 lessons or "degrees." He devised a numerical and alphabetical system called the Supreme Mathematics and Alphabet: names, numbers, and principles said to be the keys to understanding man's relationship to the universe. Young followers of the Supreme Mathematics, the Five Percenters, became known for their verbal dexterity, developed by quizzing and drilling each other on the lessons in the streets. These were the main popularizers of Black Islam among adolescents of the '60s and '70s in the New York metropolitan area—an area that includes Brooklyn and Staten Island.

THE NINE BASIC TENETS OF
THE NATION OF GODS AND EARTHS

1. That black people are the original people of the planet Earth.

2. That black people are the fathers and mothers of civilization.

3. That the science of Supreme Mathematics is the key to understanding man's relationship to the universe.

4. That Islam is a natural way of life, not a religion.

5. That education should be fashioned to enable us to be self-sufficient as a people.

6. That each one should teach one according to one's knowledge.

7. That the black man is god and his proper name is ALLAH. Arm, Leg, Leg, Arm, Head.

8. That our children are our link to the future and they must be nurtured, respected, loved, protected, and educated.

9. That the unified black family is the vital building block of the nation.

1 = **Knowledge.** That's first, because the first thing you must do is to "do the knowledge." Look, listen, observe. You walk into a party, a gunfight—look, observe. Do the knowledge.

2 = **Wisdom.** It's number two because that's the second thing you do—you do the wisdom, which is to act upon what you know. Also, wisdom is woman, because she's second to the man.

3 = **Understanding.** If you know something, and you act upon it, the next step is to truly understand it.

4 = **Culture.** After you know something, you put what you know into action, and to understand it enough to see clearly, that means you have to live it. So four is culture—the way of life. But it can also mean freedom, depending on the context.

5 = **Power.** Power is truth. The only power the devil has is power as yet unclaimed by Man.

6 = **Equality.** That's the command that you must be equal and deal equally with all people. But six is also the devil because he has the power to be equal to man, but not equal to God. Both the devil and man are physically based on six, they have six sides. But when you add knowledge to the equality you get . . .

7 = **God and perfection.** G is also the seventh letter of the alphabet, and for God. The original black man has seven and a half ounces of brain, the devil only six ounces. God sees with the seven colors of the rainbow and hears the seven notes on the musical scale.

8 = **Build.** Eight is build because God builds everything. Even the word God itself—G-O-D—you take those letters and add it up, you get eight. 7-15-4. And to build means to add on to life. And when you build positively, you take away from negativity.

9 = **Born.** To bear is to bring into existence. It takes nine months to make a baby. Nine is the only number that multiplied by itself still ends up with the same product. Nine times nine equals 81. 8 plus 1 equals 9. Why? Because nine is what brings it into existence.

0 = **Cipher, or the circle.** Because when you get to ten what happens to that ten? You're actually on the left side of that zero. You, one, are on the left side of the zero. Cipher is a zero. A circle.

A = **Allah.** Allah is the rightful name of Man, which consists of Arm, Leg, Leg, Arm, Head—A.L.L.A.H. Allah is the supreme-being original man from Asia. The sole controller and ruler of the universe, the original man who has knowledge of himself, and to know self is to know all things in existence.

B = **Be or Born.** To be born is to bring into existence physically and mentally. Just as it takes nine months to bring a child into this world, it takes nine stages to be born mentally through Allah's Mathematics.

C = **See.** To see is to understand. To understand clearly through the third eye, which is the mind. The two physical eyes are but the doorways to the third eye, which is the all-seeing eye.

D = **Divine or Destroy.** Divine is that which is holy, sacred, and pure. One must be divine in order to destroy all negativity. It also means something that is being purified from negativity.

E = **Equality.** Equality is to deal equally in all things.

F = **Father.** Father means teacher or someone who furthers another's education, one who is qualified to give life both physically and mentally.

G = **God.** God is the sole controller of the universe. He is every original black Asiatic man on the planet Earth.

H = **He or Her.** He must refine her with the knowledge of him, which is God in order to build and birth a strong foundation to carry our civilization through the her, the queen. He or She has the power to build or destroy, depending on his or her level of awareness.

I = **I or Islam.** Islam means I-Self-Lord-And-Master. It is the very nature of man and his family. Islam means peace, which is the only way of life for man, woman, and child. Islam is the only way to a positive life that will bring freedom, justice, and equality.

J = **Justice.** Justice is one's reward or penalty for one's ways or actions.

K = **King.** A king is the ruler of his entire kingdom. His word must be bond because the people look to him for guidance and intelligent instruction. It is the king who directs his people into the light of Islam.

L = **Love, Hell, or Right.** Love is supreme understanding among those who are original. Hell is the penalty for ignorance. Right is to be correct no matter who it hurts.

M = **Master.** Master is the sole controller of the universe, which is the sun, which is the Man. It is also one who has skill that will enable him to teach those with less skills, but the true master is Allah because he has 360 degrees of knowledge, wisdom, and understanding.

N = Now, Nation, or End. Now is the time for the 85 percent to knowledge their True and Divine Culture, and bring forth the power to put an end to all of their weak and wicked ways so that Man on Earth can rise and knowledge all of its creations that came from him.

O = Cipher. Cipher is the completion of a circle consisting of 360 degrees.

P = Power. Power is truth, for truth is the light, that magnetic juice that keeps the universe in fixed form, and the light is the way to be born in the kingdom of Allah.

Q = Queen. Queen is the mother of the universe; without her Islam has no future. She is the most purified woman on this earth; she must be close to the rib of man, for she was the first prize of war.

R = Rule or Ruler. God is the only ruler there is by knowledging his building powers and making them born to all the planets of the universe, so that they can go accordingly with Islam. This is bearing witness to Allah, for he is the ruler of all.

S = Self or Savior. It's like they say, "Let us save our self from the venom of the serpent."

T = Truth or Square. Truth is the only light that can stand by itself in the surroundings of darkness and yet be noticed shining in the square of the universe, which is 360 degrees.

U = You or Universe. You are the universe because we are the creators or the producers of the sun, moon, and star, and also man, woman, and child.

V = Victory. Victory comes after the war which will give Man his freedom, justice, and equality. We will have victory, this is Allah's word; surely it is the truth and light.

W = Wisdom. Wisdom is a component of knowledge, while the understanding brings about a clear picture of both through the eye of true understanding.

X = Unknown. Equality is unknown to man in North America and those who do not know themselves, the 85 percenters, who are deaf, dumb, and blind.

Y = Why. "Why?" is the question that is most frequently asked by those who are deaf, dumb, and blind. Because they don't know how to wisdom their power to show and prove their Godlyhood.

Z = Zig Zag Zig. Zig Zag Zig means knowledge, wisdom, and understanding; man, woman, and child.

- The total area of the land and water of the planet Earth is 196,940,000 square miles.
- The circumference of the planet Earth is 24,896 miles.
- The diameter of the Earth is 7,926 miles.
- The area of the Land is 57,255,000 square miles.
- The area of the Water is 139,685,000 square miles.
- The Pacific Ocean covers 68,634,000 square miles.
- The Atlantic Ocean covers 41,321,000 square miles.
- The Indian Ocean covers 29,430,000 square miles.
- The Lakes and Rivers cover 1,000,000 square miles.
- The Hills and Mountains cover 14,000,000 square miles.
- The Islands are 1,910,000 square miles.
- The Deserts are 4,861,000 square miles.
- Mount Everest is 29,141 feet high.
- The Producing Land is 29,000,000 square miles.
- The Earth weighs six sextillion tons (a unit followed by 21 ciphers).
- The Earth is 93,000,000 miles from the Sun.
- The Earth travels at the rate of $1,037\frac{1}{3}$ miles per hour.
- Light travels at the rate of 186,000 miles per second.
- Sound travels at the rate of 1,120 feet per second.
- The diameter of the Sun is 853,000 miles.

WU-TANG NUMEROLOGY

Mathematics, as we call them, describe the mechanics of the Earth. It breaks down the elements of the planet, how fast the planet spins, the speed of sound, all world history. Mathematics is at the core of the Wu-Tang Clan. U-God learned Mathematics when he was fourteen. Raekwon and I met in second grade; Meth and I met in ninth grade; GZA, Dirty, and I are cousins; and Ghost and I met in high school. So Ghost was my student. Dirty is my student. Masta Killa is GZA's student. Everybody has touched Mathematics.

You hear us use righteous terms in slang all the time. Like, "See you at the god hour" means "See you at seven o'clock." Or we call your woman "your wiz," which is short for wisdom. It's not a code, it's just that our understanding was at that level and you communicate with what you know. Some brothers have gotten mad at me for flipping the words in slang, but I'm a hip-hop slang guy, I can't help it.

Mathematics is what we live. And the numerology side of it makes you aware of the connections between everything. Even if you talk about the thirty-six chambers: A student of the Wu-Tang sword school would master higher levels of technique. Each level, or chamber, that he climbed, he would near invincibility. If he was able to enter the thirty-sixth chamber, he was unstoppable to all but a fellow thirty-sixth-chamber Wu-Tang swordsman.

So, break it down. You have the thirty-six chambers, and there's nine members of the Wu-Tang Clan. Each member of Wu-Tang has four chambers of the heart. And what's nine times four? Thirty-six. There are thirty-six fatal points on the body, and that times ten degrees of separation between each point equals 360 degrees. Therefore, the Wu-Tang Clan is a perfect circle, a cipher.

Everyone in the Wu-Tang was alert to these natural connections, even before we made an album. It was part of the power we felt as a unit.

So, around '92, I realized we had to spread Mathematics and teach the truth about what's going on in this world. So we started studying and getting more in tune with things, and started building this bond, this energy. Just prior to that year, I was living foul, a savage in my ways and actions. And I just decided to walk a straight line.

Total cost of making *Enter The Wu-Tang Clan: 36 Chambers*: $36,000.00

Β EYOND THE 120

They say a man must have 120 knowledge, 120 wisdom, and 120 understanding. That's 360 degrees total. Each 120 breaks down to a step of evolution: First you must know it, then you must be able to say it, then you must understand it. That last part, that can take ten years. The 120 covers everything that you come across in life. It goes all across world history. But basically it teaches freedom, justice, and equality. That's the foundation of Islam, but it's also what this

U-GOD USES APPLIED MATHEMATICS

I was doing a two-year penitentiary stint when they were getting ready to make *36 Chambers*. The Mathematics gave me common sense. Because before I went into jail, I was gonna be on the run—like any other black dude would have done in that situation. Like, "Oh, fuck that, I ain't going to jail." But using Mathematics, I knew that time was spinning at a certain rate and if I just gave myself up, I would come out on the other side right on time. Sure enough my calculation was right. I wound up coming out three weeks prior to the album getting ready to drop. It just so happens that I came home right on time to get on two songs on *36 Chambers*.

country is built on. They're lifelong principles throughout all history. It's just always getting fucked up by men.

For me, once I mastered my 120 lessons, I became a seeker of knowledge in general. I wanted to find the answer, the truth behind everything. The 120 is my foundation, but I started to look at it in a different way. Some brothers got mad at me about it.

People were asking, "How can you get in front of a bunch of Caucasians or Mexicans or other nationalities and talk to them like they brothers?" I said, "I gave up my shell already." Of course I bear witness to black man God Allah to take his proper place. But I don't think he's supposed to rise up in devilishment. Otherwise, are we going to take over this whole world and do the same thing, like *Planet of the Apes*?

I believe we're supposed to rise up in a different way. I believe the fundamental lesson is that everyone has the potential to become God. It's within you.

LOOK TO THE EAST

Buddha

In '93, I saw a movie called *Zen Master*. That sparked me a lot. It was the story of Da'mo, also known as Bodhidharma, the founder of Ch'an Buddhism—which became Zen Buddhism in Japan. He came around the time of Mohammed—A.D. 527, to be exact. Da'mo came from India and he walked to China and when he got there they discriminated against him. He was tall and dark. In the film they say, "He's *tall*. And he's *dark*," in this dubbed "suspicious" voice. And I was watching that thinking, "Damn, black niggas is fucked everywhere! Even the Chinese niggas is against him!"

But everything Da'mo was doing was surpassing everything in that culture. When he arrived at the Shaolin Temple, he created—based on yoga—the four seminal forms of chi gong, which became the foundation for the system of martial arts. At Shaolin, Ch'an Buddhism is martial arts and martial arts is Ch'an. Da'mo was basically teaching them about enlightenment.

After I saw that movie, I started reading the *Tao Te Ching* and the *I Ching*. I was looking for the common thread of knowledge between what was going on then and now. I started to get more observant of what I was causing to happen and what was causing me to cause it. The lessons opened my mind up.

THE "THREE WAYS": TAOISM, BUDDHISM, CONFUCIANISM

Lao Tzu

The *Tao* means, basically, the "Way." It refers to the flow of life, the way nature expresses itself. Taoism teaches you to unite your actions with the flow of the universe. You want to be spontaneous and free from outside influences like social institutions. Confucianism, on the other hand, is more like a concept of government, conduct, and social order. So they seem like opposites, but in Chinese society, they—along with Buddhism—combine to form a general approach to the world.

Confucianism is about relationships. Buddhism is

about release. Taoism is about balance. If your life is in turmoil and conflict, you're not living in the Tao.

I got sparked on this when I met Sifu. It was in 1995, at a record release party for GZA's *Liquid Swords.* Sifu Shi Yan-Ming is a thirty-fourth-generation monk from the Shaolin Temple in China. He defected to the U.S. in 1992 and founded his own Shaolin temple in Manhattan. We became friends, and I became a student. That's when the Wu-Tang Clan became humble warriors.

We weren't humble warriors in the beginning. Before, we would always say, "We ain't about flipping and kicking, we'll flip lyrics and kick your ass." But now we started to see the truth of it. When Sifu came to us, I think destiny brought it to us. Then we had a living example of the actual principles. I learned that kung fu was less a fighting style and more about the cultivation of the spirit.

ODB and I started to get deep into what they were saying about chi energy. We got into the idea of channeling chi. It rejuvenates your body, but it's also philosophical. It's about finding balance.

Chi is the life force. It's the same thing as Prana in the Hindu religion. (My daughter's name is Prana.) Balancing your chi is in a lot of ways about putting your actions in place with the universe.

Confucius

The *Tao Te Ching* teaches of three jewels, or characteristics, that man should cherish. They are Compassion, which leads to courage, Moderation, which leads to generosity, and Humility, which leads to leadership.

Confucianism was basically a wisdom of warriors. I studied Confucius maybe more around 1996, I got deeper into him. It's like rules of conduct. But they both go together.

One basic element of Chinese religions is that they see

all religions as part of a whole. Confucianism and Taoism are related, they're like yin and yang in some ways. A lot of people see life in terms of opposites—like, good versus evil, me versus you, valuable versus worthless. Taoists believe you have to see beyond the opposites, to find the real unity among all things.

I think if you talk to everybody in the crew and ask them why they're humble now, they'd say it's because they felt the need to achieve balance. Once you have knowledge of yourself,

The Wu-Tang Clan meets Sifu for the first time at *Liquid Swords* record release party.

you'll seek balance consciously. If you don't seek balance yourself, life will balance you. That's why a lot of niggas go to jail, go through hell. When Wu-Tang first came in, we were so threatening. Now you can see we've all humbled ourselves down a little. We understand you need silent weapons for quiet wars.

Today, I'm not a Muslim. I'm not a Buddhist. I'm not a soldier of any one religious sect. I realized you can never put a circle around the truth and say that it belongs to one sect. I'm a student. Like Solomon said, "He sought wisdom out from the cradle to the grave."

I would say the only religion I practice now is universal love. People fight and kill each other and say they have the proper remedy to give it to you, but nobody can *give* it to you. You have to recognize it within yourself. My way of life is Islam. But there's an acronym they use for Islam which is I, Self, Lord, And Master. Or, I like to say, I Stimulate Light And Matter. You have to realize that *you* stimulate everything around you. Everything else is only a reflection.

THE WAY OF THE WU:
THE RAZOR-SHARP SUTRA

You can break Ch'an Buddhism down to three basic ideas. One is that every person has an inherent Buddha nature inside—anyone can become enlightened. Two, there's no one single path to enlightenment, everybody has to find his own way. Three, it's almost impossible to reach enlightenment solely through the exchange of words.

In 1999, I went with Sifu to the other Shaolin, the one in China. I went to the original Shaolin Temple, the birthplace of kung fu. It's over fifteen hundred years old. I got to be the first MC to perform there. When we went to Shaolin, Sifu said to me, "This is your home. Welcome home." He doesn't always speak great English, but it's like what he says, I already know.

RZA receives the other Wu-Tang music.

On that trip, we also went to Wu-Tang Mountain in Hebei Province. That's where I met the Abbot of the *other* Wu-Tang. He hit me with a tape of music from their Wu-Tang. I can't really describe what that trip was like other than to say one word: Enlightenment.

The most important sutra is called the Diamond Sutra. They call it that because the wisdom that's contained in this sutra could cut diamonds—that's how laser-sharp it is. And that sutra says, "'What do you have to teach, Buddha?' And Buddha says, 'I have nothing to teach.'" You have to learn it on your own.

MARTIAL ARTS

When you see a swordsman, draw your sword. Do not recite poetry to one who is not a poet.

—CH'AN BUDDHIST PROVERB

"Shaolin shadowboxing, and the Wu-Tang sword style

If what you say is true, the Shaolin and the Wu-Tang

could be dangerous"

"Do you think your Wu-Tang sword can defeat me?"

"En garde,! I'll let you try my Wu-Tang style"

I read this book *The Five Chinese Brothers* when I was a kid and it really fascinated me—one brother swallowed the sea, one had an iron neck, one couldn't be burned. I don't know what it was, but something about their powers, the way they worked together—it stuck

There are five Chinese brothers, each endowed with a special power or ability. The first one is able to swallow the entire ocean. When he helps a young boy fish by draining the sea, the boy fails to heed his call to return from the dry seabed and drowns when the sea is released. The brother is condemned to decapitation for this crime, but sends his second brother to the execution. This brother has a neck of iron that cannot be chopped off. The remaining brothers foil successive attempts at execution, each by employing his own unique talent until the case is dropped.

with me. So when I finally saw a trailer for the *The Five Deadly Venoms,* I thought, "Oh, they made a movie about those cats?" The seed had been planted long ago. From the point that I saw that movie, it was on.

I got my introduction to kung-fu flicks in '78 or '79. You'd get a triple feature on Forty-second Street for $1.50. At that point, all of Forty-second Street had kung-fu movies. They'd have three on this side of the street and another three on the other side and they'd rotate them. They'd play them with regular first-run movies. Any given night, you could see *Fright Night, Motel Hell, Invasion of the Bodysnatchers*–plus two kung-fu flicks.

So this first one I saw was *The Chinese Mack*–the character was like a pimp. *The Mack* had been a popular movie in the hood so they came up with that name to sell it to the U.S. The other one was *The Fist of Double-K.*

But it wasn't until I saw *The Five Deadly Venoms*–by the Shaw Brothers, in 1979–that I was really hooked. After that, I was a movie-goer every week. I was sucked in. I cut school for it, it became obsessive. I didn't think it got any better than *The Five Deadly Venoms*, but then another movie took me to a whole other level.

I was maybe fourteen years old and on TV they'd play a Bruce Lee movie and then advertise a kung-fu flick afterwards. This time, they played *Bruce Lee: The True Story,* and at the end they said, "Coming next week, June 6: *The Thirty-sixth Chamber.*" It was like a magic moment. I remember that ad to this day. It was June 6: 36. Six–six–thirty-six.

This movie might have been made in 1979, but it was a period piece, based on a true story. It's about this guy San-Te who became a Shaolin monk. First the guy knows nothing, then slowly, painfully, he masters the whole thirty-five chambers in seven years. After he mastered all the levels, he wanted to start a thirty-sixth chamber, which was to teach the knowledge of Shaolin to the rest of the world. But the monks don't believe they belong to the world, so they exile him. But the abbot who exiled him knew that the ones who became the thirty-six chamber students were going to come after him.

I was just amazed by this movie—the action, the moves, the period, and the message it was giving—it was just sublime. On the surface, it was about a revolution against the Manchus. You had the government oppressing all the people, but the young didn't even know that they were oppressed. So this schoolteacher was teaching his students about sacrifice and righteousness and the students ask him if he'd been to the hanging they just had out in town. They're all laughing, and he says, "I'd be laughing if it was the *Manchus* that were hanging." Suddenly, these students realize the truth. They didn't know they were oppressed, they figured that's how it's always been. I could relate to that on a lot of levels.

The second part of the movie was the training he went through to become a master, to build himself up. That part took me by storm. I actually began doing push-ups and punching walls, going to Chinatown and getting books, the whole trip.

The Thirty-sixth Chamber was the one that opened my mind. The idea of self-discipline, of re-creating yourself. I was around fourteen years old. And it changed me, for real.

THE 36TH CHAMBER AKA: MASTER KILLER (1978)

Gordon Liu stars as a Chinese fugitive from the Manchu invaders who hides out at the Shaolin kung-fu temple, trains in its arts, and introduces kung fu to the oppressed people of China—ultimately becoming the legendary monk San Te. It was directed by real-life Shaolin student Lau Kar-Leung, who brought an unprecedented degree of real martial artistry to film. At least half of this film is about training, following the hero's growth from lowly refugee, through his punishing regime of menial chores, and on to his study in the thirty-five chambers of Shaolin mastery. The rest of the film focuses on San Te's foundation of his own thirty-sixth chamber, in which he will share his knowledge with the world and lead an army against the Manchu.

ENTER THE PROJECTS: PARK HILL VS. STAPLETON

Park Hill was known for fly niggas and Stapleton was known for stick-up niggas. Park Hill niggas will shoot you, but Stapleton niggas will rob you and beat the shit out of you. A Park Hill nigga will pull up in a Benz, get out looking good, and pull a gun out. A Stapleton nigga will walk up to you with a fucking tank top and a doorag on and fuck you up. It's better to get jacked by a Park Hill nigga because a Stapleton nigga gonna whup your ass, too. Of course, that's just in my generation. In the earlier generation, they said it was the opposite. So things go in cycles. Yin and yang.

About three years after I saw *The Thirty-sixth Chamber*, I was still going to kung-fu flicks, mostly with Dirty. We'd go to a twenty-four-hour movie spot that showed pornos and kung-fu flicks. By that time it was mostly porno on Forty-second Street, but some of the porno places had a small room, maybe the size of a classroom, where bums would sleep and they'd show these kung-fu flicks.

So ODB and I, we were always out at night around Times Square—starting fights, getting drunk, chasing women, going to the Roseland—and this one night, we were really high, we'd been out all night and didn't want to go home. It was cold and we had a couple of 40-ounces and we thought we'd crash at this funky theater at Forty-second Street and Seventh Avenue.

So we went in, at maybe four in the morning, and sat down to watch whatever was on. Some we had seen before, but there was one that we'd never seen: *Shaolin and Wu-Tang*. We walked in near the end of it, and just from the last few minutes I was like, "What the fuck is this?" It ended and another movie came on and we watched that, and Dirty wanted to leave. But I was like "I got to see that movie." We stayed and when it came on, it woke us up. It was the best kung-fu movie I'd ever seen in my life—the fighting, the ideas, the concepts, everything.

I'd never seen that kind of sword fighting in movies before—they made it so beautiful. But something about the Wu-Tang attitude really sparked me, too. The Wu-Tang sword style was invincible and when the Wu fights the Shaolin monks and defeats them—beats like thirty guys—he gets expelled. But when he's expelled, he says, "I may have been expelled but I'm still the best—Wu-*Tang*!" In a way, it was like the devil in the Bible: a powerful angel that got a swelled head and got banished. He may be kicked out, but he knows he's bad.

The Wu-Tang were the *bad* guys in a lot of these movies. As you watch more and you notice more, you realize, for example, in *The White Lotus*, those bad guys are the Wu-Tang people. Even in *Kill Bill: Vol. 2*, Pai Mei—he's Wu-Tang. In a lot of movies, the bad guys the Shaolin were fighting were the Wu-Tang because the government hired the Wu-Tang. They conformed. They realized that the times were changing. They were survivalists.

Years later, around '89, Wu-Tang fever was sweeping through the projects. It hit videotape and everyone in the neighborhood was hooked on it. We just started watching it at my house playing hooky. By 1990, it was a slang phrase: "Wu-Tang" was just something that was fly as far as the street level of it. It was happening mostly in Stapleton Projects—with me and Ghostface, we were roommates and partners. And other young guys were using it as slang, too.

One of the most acclaimed of all kung-fu films, directed and choreographed by Kar Leung and starring Gordon Liu in a tale of the Mongols' campaign to defeat the the Sung Dynasty. The film begins with an ambush led by the traitorous Sung general, played by Pai Mei, against the famed family of warrior brothers, the Yangs. The attack kills all but two of the brothers and their father. One brother is left insane while the last goes on to infiltrate a kung-fu monastery to improve his pole fighting abilities and take revenge.

The last movie that formed the Wu-Tang Clan brotherhood is called *The Eight Diagram Pole Fighter.* That was a movie I saw on tape for the first time with my brothers and sisters. It was a movie about eight brothers who get betrayed, go to war, and many get killed. And my family has eight brothers. I have three sisters and there are three sisters in the movie. So my whole family watched that movie over and over and over. This movie was very special to my family.

So later, once everyone at the projects was fiended out on kung fu—all cutting class, coming to the crib, and watching videos, I decided to show them this one, *The Eight Diagram Pole Fighter. Wu-Tang* was good for the moves and fighting and the sword style. But *The Eight Diagram Pole Fighter* is the story of brotherhood.

So this one day, about eight or nine of us—me, Ghost, and a bunch of Stapleton niggas—are getting high and I put on the movie. Not too long into it, something deep happened. People start feeling it. Some niggas even started crying.

Because that movie is *real.* It's a kung-fu movie, but it's a real story. These eight brothers who go out and they get betrayed and they fight to the death for each other—it hit us. And niggas was saying, "I'm the Fifth Brother!" "I'm the Sixth Brother!" They were relating to it on that level. So we started calling each other by the names of those brothers.

I think what got them was the betrayal and the brotherhood. The general betrays the whole family, and the father gets killed, and all the brothers get killed except for two. One goes crazy and the other gets a chance to be a monk. And he goes and cuts his hair to do it. That scene where this guy cuts his hair . . . Believe me, it's real.

Listen, we're oppressed. It does feel like we as a people were betrayed a long time ago. I can't really describe it any other way. It's real because the issues are alive with us. You're living in the hood and you've got knowledge and dreams and you got wars between neighborhood and neighborhood and neighborhood. Everybody's backstabbing everybody. And when you know someone who's got your back, that's a life-or-death thing. That's a real bond, a real brotherhood.

Everybody was into the kung-fu films, but I don't know if everybody really knew the true meaning of what we were dealing with, the *true* meaning of it. I did. Ghostface did. I think that GZA did. Dirty did. And we basically had to educate the rest of the guys on the philosophy. Ghost was the first one to say, "*That's* Wu-Tang. *I'm* Wu-Tang."

So in our case, it breaks down like this: From *The Thirty-sixth Chamber* you get discipline and struggle. From *Shaolin and Wu-Tang,* you get the virtuosity, the invincible style and technique–plus, the idea that sometimes the bad guys are the illest. And from *Eight Diagram Pole Fighter*, you get the brotherhood, the soul.

I was a Mathematician and a deep knowledge person. By this time, I recognized the dialogue, what it meant. I realized that Shaolin was the foundation of Wu-Tang. Shaolin is your mind and Wu-Tang is your body. You could be Wu-Tang, and Shaolin is where you come from. That's why I named Staten Island Shaolin. We are Wu-Tang and we come from Shaolin.

Wu-Tang was the best sword style. And with us, our tongue is our sword. So I was like, "The book and the sword are the two things that control the world. We either gonna control them through knowledge and influence their minds, or we gonna bring the sword and take their heads off." That's why we called our first joint "Protect Ya Neck." And that's why I kept the Wu-Tang as the name of our group. I said, "Wu-Tang is us. We are the Wu-Tang Clan. Clan means family. We family now."

The first logo my man Mathematics did was the guy holding a head by the dreadlocks (see page 41). That one was too gory, but I liked how he wrote the letters, so I had him come up with the sword—because my tongue is my sword. But that didn't reflect everything I was about either. So I told him it needs to represent the sword, the book, and the wisdom. It's like you either go with the book, and have it peaceful, or you got the sword. That's the same idea of the Muslim flag's sword. It's saying, "We gave you the knowledge, the Holy Koran, and we'll cut your fucking head off if you act savage."

So then the logo was the book, with the W on it, and the sword underneath. As time went on I removed the book and the sword, and left the W. The W looks like a sword, but it's also like a bat raising up or a raven or a phoenix. Plus it had some Batman flavor. Not that I meant it to—but it didn't hurt.

MARTIAL
ARTS

Wu-Tang were known for their internal martial arts and their exquisite swordplay. We felt that the tongue, as Caesar said, is a double-edged sword. And so Wu-Tang declared, "Our lyrics are the best—we're invincible."

So we took a martial arts approach to that and said we're using a Wu-Tang style. We always apply that to the music: the warrior aspect, the brotherhood of the art, the challenge of it. Because samurais and swordsmen always walk up and challenge each other and duel. An MC battle is like that to us—a challenge of the sword. We apply that to everything we do—from the sound of it, to the competitive swordplay of the rhyming, to the mental preparations.

The ultimate goal of kung fu, the highest level of t'ai chi as an effective martial art, is as an energy rejuvenator. It rejuvenates your blood, your spirit, it's even supposed to rejuvenate your youth. When we applied the spirit of kung fu to our lyrics, we came with the Wu-Tang.

Box in Hand—A training technique in which the student is to attempt to snatch a box from the master's hand.

Crane Style—A system in which the fighter keeps his arms wide, makes winglike movements, uses high kicking, and employs the crane's beak—a hand weapon made by joining the fingertips tightly together.

Dragon Style—A mercurial style that begins hard and external, and changes into a flowing, defensive art. Its intent is to tire the opponent out by stopping his blows and attack with deceptively fluid gestures.

Drunk Style—During the Tang dynasty Shaolin warriors saved the life of Emperor Li Shimin, and an imperial decree allowed Shaolin monks to drink wine. Since they rarely had, some Shaolin monks became drunk. After some observation of this, one decided that the actions of a drunk person could be used in a powerful new style. Thus they developed Drunk Style—using the slow and sloppy movements of a drunk person to deceive and create a great force for each blow.

Eagle Style—A Shaolin technique derived from the swooping of an eagle after its prey. It uses swift hits from both the hands and legs.

Leopard Style—An intermediate of the Tiger Style (see Tiger Style), it has several major offensive techniques: the chain and whip, and the leopard fist. The fist is used to jab and rake along soft spots on the anatomy. It is an offenive style meant to injure an opponent.

Mantis Style—A technique based on arm and finger strength, which the fighter develops to the point he can pierce stone. Legend has it the style was inspired by a preying mantis's ability to fight off a hawk.

Monkey Style—A technique whose offensive and defensive positions are meant to surprise and disorient an enemy. This style is the first mastered style of a child monk, who is usually initiated by age ten.

Serpent Style—A technique of kung-fu terrorism, used primarily to scare the opponent with the force of tremendously quick, injury-inflicting jabs on pressure points, some of which cause severe internal bleeding but are not life threatening.

Shadow Box—1. To spar with an imaginary opponent. 2. A form of Shaolin fighting where the hands move extremely quickly, like the flick of a shadow.

Tiger Style—A hard external style that meets force with force. Its primary hand weapons are the closed fist and the tiger claw, while the kicking manuevers are usually low- to middle-range kicks of extreme power. The key to the style is the strong counterattack.

RZA and Sifu in China.
Wu-Tang Mountain is
behind them.

I never really got seriously into one special kung-fu style, but I definitely got the basic foundation for how to get your body healthy. I learned a few breathing exercises to help rejuvenate the body. At the same time, because I read so many books and watched so many films, I felt like I had a natural instinct for a certain reflex.

Sifu Shi Yan-Ming

Then when we met Sifu, the real Shaolin monk, me, Ghostface, and GZA started taking chi-gong training with him. It's stretching, breathing, and Shaolin training—getting our bodies in shape. It's not so much punching and kicking but it involves different postures. What made a Shaolin monk so tough was his mastery of chi. He could make contact with the Earth and draw the energy from it through him.

As I got further into the game and the industry, I started to look at the martial arts in a broader context. Lyor Cohen, from Def Jam, gave me the book *The Prince* by Machiavelli. And there were other older artists who'd drop that stuff on you. *The Art of War* by Sun Tzu—lots of cats in the industry got into that. Way back, that helped me out in my business and my life. It's also a beautiful book. I went from that to *The Art of Peace, The Sword of the Mind,* all the ninja stuff. That was when I started reading the *Tao Te Ching,* the *I Ching, The Hagakure.* It all helped me out in my business and my life.

This was '92, '93, I'd already had my experience in the industry, from being the solo artist. So I was reading books on the industry and these martial principles. I also read this one book, *Secret Art of War: The 36 Stratagems*—obviously I had to get *that* one. It was written after Sun Tzu, near the end of the Ming Dynasty—a lot of it is about deception and countermoves, methods of attack.

Those books applied to my business knowledge and my street knowledge. I knew that if I took a certain path I could reach certain goals.

Lord Naoshige said, "The Way of the Samurai is in desperateness. Ten men or more cannot kill such a man. Common sense will not accomplish great things. Simply become insane and desperate."

— THE HAGAKURE

One thing that made the Wu-Tang Clan humble warriors was that, individually, we had been cool most of our lives. I mean, we had desperate periods, and out of one desperate situation arose the Wu-Tang Clan. But as teenagers we were already fly.

For example, I went to the Polo store the other day and I was laughing, looking at the shelves. All these clothes I'd already had. When I was sixteen, I had a car already, more jewelry than I wear now—I'd already gone through that. We were the beautiful motherfuckers—the niggas other niggas made songs about.

But as time went on, we got backed into a corner. We did get desperate. And that was when the Wu-Tang Clan really started to take shape. We had that hunger, that need to learn martial arts, to learn all that shit—to survive. There's no better motivation than that.

THE 36 STRATAGEMS

I. Stratagems when in a superior position

Cross the sea under camouflage

Besiege Wei to rescue Zhao

Kill with a borrowed knife

Wait at ease for the fatigued enemy

Loot a burning house

Make a feint to the east while attacking in the west

II. Stratagems for confrontation

Create something out of nothing

Advance to Chencang by a hidden path

Watch the fire burning across the river

Conceal a dagger in a smile

Sacrifice plums for peaches

Take a goat in passing

III. Stratagems for attack

Beat the grass to startle the snake

Raise a corpse from the dead

Lure the tiger out of the mountain

Let the enemy off in order to snare him

Cast a brick to attract a gem

To capture rebels, capture their leader

IV. Stratagems for confused situations

Take away the fire from under the cauldron

Fish in troubled waters

The cicada sheds its skin

Bolt the door to catch the thief

Befriend a distant state while attacking a neighbor

Borrow a route to conquer Guo

V. Stratagems for gaining ground

Replace the beams and pillars with rotten timber

Point at the mulberry only to curse the locust

Feign foolishness

Remove the ladder after the ascent

Put fake blossoms on the tree

Reverse host and guest

VI. Stratagems for desperate situations

Scheme with beauties

Scheme with an empty castle

Sow discord in the enemy's camp

Inflict injury on oneself to win the enemy's trust

Scheme in continuous circles

Know when retreat is the best option

CAPITALISM

"This is one of our nation's great companies, and one of the most familiar names in all of America. The story of [this company] exemplifies some of the very best qualities in our country—hard work, the spirit of enterprise, fair dealing, and integrity."

—VICE PRESIDENT DICK CHENEY,

IN A SPEECH TO EMPLOYEES OF WAL-MART, MAY 3, 2004

During a three-year hiatus after their 1997 record-setting double album *Wu-Tang Forever*, the group's Wu-Wear clothing line hit $15 million in annual sales, the comic book line nudged out *X-Men* for the top spot in the country, and its first kung-fu video game sold 600,000 units for Sony PlayStation. And six Clan members recorded successful solo albums.

—*TIME* MAGAZINE

The Wu is too slammin for these Cold Killin labels
Some ain't had hits since I seen Aunt Mabel
Be doin artists in like Cain did Abel
Now they money's gettin stuck to the gum under the table

—GZA, "PROTECT YA NECK,"

ENTER THE WU-TANG: 36 CHAMBERS

THE AWAKENING

The most basic economic lesson you get doing music is your first show as a group. Do a show, get a hundred bucks, split it down to ten dollars apiece. That puts things in perspective. But GZA and I had our experiences in the industry as solo artists before Wu-Tang even started, so we had the toughest teacher you can have: reality. In a way, we were ready.

In 1991 Ghostface and I were roommates in the Stapleton Projects when we started running around with this Wu-Tang idea. Meanwhile, in Park Hill—that's where Method Man, Raekwon, and Inspectah Deck are from—they were calling themselves the DMD crew, for Dick 'Em Down. I started hanging out more in Park Hill, with Method Man, and I told him about this idea of Wu-Tang, not as a recording group, but as a crew. Then it started spreading around.

I was with Tommy Boy back then. The single I had been working, "Ooh, I Love You Rakeem," was dead already. I told Tommy Boy I wanted to change my name to Wu-Tang and come in with this crew—at that point, me, Ghost, Meth, and U-God.

At first, Tommy Boy said they'd do it. In fact, there was actually an ad in *The Source* in 1991 that lists their roster on the back cover, and at the bottom, you see "Wu-Tang Clan." Tommy Boy could have had Wu-Tang but they never signed the deal. They made the decision to sign House of Pain over us.

When they dropped me, I was thinking, "Damn, they chose a bunch of whiteboy shit over me." I felt bamboozled. I started getting back into the street life and got into some trouble, had to go out of state.

VISIONZ

Only those thoughts that come by walking have any value.

—FRIEDRICH NIETZSCHE

In April 1991, I came back to New York. That was a dark time. I walked the street for months, strategizing, pondering what to do next. Finally I decided to form a production company. I studied music industry books and taught myself how to get into the business.

I was sure that if I walked this path that my mind had set in front of me, I was going to the top, and nothing was going stop me. I walked around for three months contemplating before I formed my company. Then I contemplated for three more months on who I wanted with me. The Clan was formed only in principle and in street credibility, not in legal or business terms.

I spent May, June, and July just walking. I used to walk for miles. Either from Park Hill or Stapleton to the ferry area, or the Port Richmond area to the park, or New Brighton to Stapleton. Staten Island—it's pretty big, so you can get some good walks in. I need to walk. I do it still, to think. Even now, I go to Staten Island, park my car, and walk. I travel that same path that I traveled so many times as a kid.

Back then, I remember this one girl who used to see me out there walking from her window. She said, "We used to think you were crazy. We'd see you out there, walking, talking to yourself." I told her, "I wasn't talking to myself. But I probably was talking."

First of all, who's your A&R?
A mountain climber who plays an electric guitar
But he don't know the meaning of dope
When he's lookin for a suit and tie rap
That's cleaner than a bar of soap
And I'm the dirtiest thing in sight
Matter of fact bring out the girls and let's have a mud fight

—GZA, "PROTECT YA NECK,"
ENTER THE WU-TANG: 36 CHAMBERS

In 1992, I formed Wu-Tang Productions. By this time, we were all still known as the Wu-Tang—even Dirty and GZA were calling themselves Wu-Tang, though they were in Brooklyn. So we had the name, but we still didn't have a group. It's funny, you see that later with the dot-com companies claiming domain names before they even have a company.

At that point, me and Ghost wanted to come out as Wu-Tang, but no one wanted to pitch in. So we just did it ourselves, the two of us, and we recorded "After the Laughter." That was the first Wu-Tang song.

At the time, something started happening in me. I had this burning sensation in my head, like: I'm not stopping. I thought, let me go to my homies and get them all involved. So the next people I stepped to were Meth and Inspectah Deck. They were on the block doing their thing, involved with negativity. I pulled up on them and told them, "I'm gonna get some contracts and bring them to y'all and I want y'all to join my record company. I'm gonna get you off these streets." And they said, "Yo, to get me off these streets, anything."

They signed and we recorded some songs. Popularity started floating around the neighborhood. That's when I had the idea for "Protect Ya Neck." I wanted to get the best MCs, the whole crew, and record a song.

I called everybody and told them to meet me at the studio. Everyone was supposed to bring fifty dollars to pay for the session. When we got there, some of the MCs didn't want to pay or didn't have the money. Ghost said, "That nigga don't wanna pay fifty dollars? Fuck that nigga." I told him not to worry, that I'd put up their money.

We marketed the single, "Protect Ya Neck/After the Laughter" from my basement. We pressed five hundred copies and sold it directly to record stores and DJs. This was *before* the Internet and the whole direct-to-buyer explosion. After that started a buzz, I knew we could bargain from a position of strength. That was when I told everyone about my plan.

THE FIVE-YEAR PLAN

After we recorded "Protect Ya Neck" and it started blowing up, I knew that we had to form one big crew officially. There were eight of us at this point, everyone except for Masta Killa. Although everyone agreed to join up, most didn't want to sign contracts. So I told them about my vision.

Five years. I told them that the next five years would be guided by the force of will and that for those five years I was the answer. There was a certainty that nothing could hold us back. I would tempt death because I knew I couldn't die. I told them that if they'd put their solo careers on hold, we could work together for something much bigger. I told them, "If y'all give me five years of your life, I promise you in five years I'm gonna take us to the top." And so we gave each other our word. The Wu-Tang Clan was born.

THE ART OF THE DEAL

The deals we made are famous now. Not one other group had our kind of strategy. My idea was to keep the family together, sign the Wu-Tang as a crew to one label, but have the contract allow the individual members to sign solo deals on whatever labels they chose. You bargain for less money up front, more freedom in the longer run, and higher earnings total.

The goal was to divide ourselves and conquer the record industry. Most rap niggas weren't thinking like that back then, looking multiple moves ahead. The contract we signed with Loud in 1993 changed the way hip-hop artists negotiate, the way deals are structured; it changed the whole rap game. But in reality, some of the deals I made were stupid. They're famous now because they worked.

In the music business, in reality, it's usually best to keep all your artists under one umbrella because you get a bigger payday. But I wanted my artists under many umbrellas because I wanted the industry to work for me. I wanted the industry to have friendly competition with my product, without even knowing they were competing with each other. And then I'd bring them together for the final moneymaker.

That was my original strategy—to have artists placed in different locations and get those different labels to work together for my brand. Of course I learned that's not easy to do, because the labels are always in competition with one another and don't always want to cooperate when you want them to.

There was only one year, 1995, that they all listened to me, and that turned out to be a great year for everybody. I came with the "Winter Campaign"—I said, "Let's do a Christmas Wu-Tang family tree, put them all at one location." So we did. Geffen, Loud, Def Jam, and Elektra got together and put a bin in record stores with the GZA record, the Wu-Tang record, the Method Man record, and so on. Everybody sells double that month. It was the first time that three different labels made a triple deal together. That's how my logo, my brand, became the strongest brand in the industry.

> Wu-Tang Incorp. take your brain on spacewalk
> Talk strange like B-jork, great hero Jim Thorpe
> . . . I got the golden egg plus the goose
> Eighty proof, Absolut, mixed with cranberry fruit juice
> Ginseng boost, I got yo' neck in a noose
> Keep my money wrinkled, the rap star twinkle killer instinct
> sixteen bar nickle sell more copies than Kinko
> Grow like a fetus with no hands and feet to complete us
> and we return like Jesus, when the whole world need us
>
> —RZA, "REUNITED," *WU-TANG FOREVER*

In a way it was like a war, it was like a mafia movie, it was like a kung-fu epic—for a while, it was everything. My brother Divine is my business manager, he's like my consigliere. He's like me, but in some ways he's exactly opposite of me. Some call us night and day. And then we had my man, Power. The three of us were the business mind of Wu-Tang.

A lot of my business plans definitely come from *The 36 Stratagems*, but they also come just from who I am and the people I work with. The business works with the weight of the artists holding the weight of the whole situation and still getting pimped by the industry. I didn't do that. I wasn't just putting some rap niggas on my shit and putting it out. These were motherfuckers I grew up with. Also, I'm patient. I can wait till the end to get mine. You make a sacrifice in the beginning for the long-term reward. It's not only going to benefit us, it's going to benefit our artists, our seeds, everyone.

The ultimate aim of my long-term plan was to take over one-third of the industry. I counted how many hip-hop artists there were and how many artists I had and I realized that we could do it. We had someone in our fold to compete with anyone that was out there. You could go down the line. We had Meth, Ghost, Rae, RZA, and then we had Sunz Of Man, Killarmy, Royal Fam—who are still some of the best MCs, they just never got their full shine.

So I figured that by a certain year, one-third of hip-hop would be governed by me. That was a long-term plan—like a seven-to-ten-year plan. My five-year plan was to take the energy of the Wu-Tang Plan, under the dictatorship of me and my idea, and in five years we'd be number one.

It happened. In 1997, when *Wu-Tang Forever* came out, we were the number one group—in sales, influence, everything. We sold 600,000 units the first week, the phenomenon made CNN. This was with no radio, no hit single, no nothing.

W U   W E A R

Every morning, the samurai of fifty or sixty years ago would bathe, shave their foreheads, put lotion in their hair, cut their fingernails and toenails rubbing them with pumice and then with wood sorrel, and without fail pay attention to their personal appearance. It goes without saying that their armor in general was kept free from rust, that it was dusted, shined, and arranged.

– THE HAGAKURE

We started Wu Wear in 1995 when we had the money. We weren't the first hip-hop group to come out with our own clothing line. Naughty, for one thing, did it with Naughty Wear. But we definitely did it to the utmost.

Some of it was business, but it was also about style and filling a need. I knew that how we dressed and how we looked was what it was. I knew that nobody would make exactly what I wanted. Even though I loved Polo and Tommy Hilfiger, they weren't making a lot of Double-XLs. It'd be just L or XL. It was more whiteboy shit.

Most pants at that time were definitely whiteboy shit. All the baggy pants by Cross Colours was all nerd-looking. We started taking the styles that we actually wore—like the army fatigue pants, but with the drawstrings at the front and drawstrings at the bottom of your pants—and told tailors how to make them. That's what we wanted. When Wu-Wear first started, my man Power, he's Executive Producer Oli Grant, went and got tailors and had them make all our clothes for the first year.

We'd have old pants, like three years old, and we'd tell them, "Make shit like this, but make this like *this*—pleat the jeans up one level, don't make it tight like that," and so on.

WU GUIDELINES FOR THE PROPER ROCKING OF GEAR

Pants—Basically we want eight inches at the bottom of the leg for an average guy; skinny guy, six inches. Waist: 38—no matter how skinny you are. I'm skinnier than skinny and I start with 38. Thirty-eight—that's where it's at.

Shirt—You want the sleeve to come down by your knuckles. If you want to show your watch, you roll up the cuff. But we wasn't into showing off watches back then, just rings. The sleeves gotta hang. The size should be basically XXL, no matter what size you are. Basically, you want to think 17, 34 is the size shirt. 17–17$\frac{1}{2}$, 34—you start with that and go up from there.

T-Shirt—Usually we rock a T-shirt longer than the shirt we're wearing over it because we like to wear layers. Make it red, yellow, blue—maybe make the colors match parts of your sneakers to make it even iller.

Accessories—You got your doorags, your wristbands. We'd also rock two headbands of two different colors. We kind of started that. Two wristbands on each arm.

Shoes—Timberland boots or Wallabees really. That's about it.

Domewear—New York Yankee ballcaps is the standard, but any cool cap that fits your head right. Try to stay away from the ones with the strap on the back. Some of those come with Velcro straps. Velcro straps are better than the button strap and the slider is better than the Velcro.

You gotta bend your brim. Nowadays, you see guys rock it with a straight brim, way up on the top of their heads. It's what I call Cleveland style. They're doing their thing, that's just not how we get down. Back in the day, lots of motherfuckers bent the brim til was like a C-shape. I remember Ghost, he used to bend that motherfucker so he'd get a V out of it.

You can rock a hat at different angles, but I rock it straight. But any hat *besides* a baseball hat? That, you gotta tilt in some way. Any other hat, tilt that motherfucker. Then you'll be aight.

I never got too hung up on what exact kinds of products Wu-Wear sold—that was more Power's department. To me, the W can go on anything. But when they came with all the different Wu colognes, with flavors for different members, that stopped me for a minute. I walked into the store one day and I was like "Yo, who the fuck said this was *my* flavor?" I think they took Blue Nile and Egyptian Musk and mixed them together and that was the RZA scent. Then again, that's what I used to wear as a teenager—Egyptian Musk, Blue Nile, and Opium, so I guess it made sense.

And the thing is, it all worked. Every little gadget they put that W on, it sold.

THE INTEGRITY OF THE W

Virtual Corporation: A temporary network of independent companies linked by telecommunications to share skills, costs, and access to one another's markets.

—BUSINESS WEEK

On Ghostface Killer's *Supreme Clientele,* you see the production is credited to the RZA and Ghostface. But we got beats from a whole bunch of niggas—Carlos Broady, Juju of the Beatnuts, Hassan of UMC's, Mo the Barber, Black Moe's Art. After the niggas gave us a beat, we'd never seen them again. But that's the way we wanted to try doing it. Usually, a producer comes in and he makes the beat, mixes it, guides the whole path of it. But nobody did that for this album but me and Ghost. That's why it has a special sound.

Today, Wu-Tang Corp, as we call it, is linked to at least thirty companies. I started a joint venture company with Brian Haberline and Aaron Bullock, the ones who did the comic *Spawn*, for the Wu-Tang comic book. We did the video game, *Wu-Tang: Shaolin Style*. I'm investing in some film coming out. I got a slew of music coming out, always.

I'm moving more toward looking at the integrity of the brand. My outlook isn't really about how much revenue we're making right now. The purity of the W is more where my heart is at.

A few years ago I used to say we're going to take this from digital to Disney. Wu-Tang is going to be like the Mickey Mouse ears. And we've done that to some extent, but along the way, some partners we joined up with didn't have the same agenda as we had for our logo.

So now, I'm just going back to the integrity of the W. Of course we're going make money when the next record comes out and there'll be more opportunities, but I'm not prepared to jump at every opportunity. It's got to be within the integrity of our brand.

Reunited, double LP, we're all excited
Struck a match to the underground, industry ignited
From metaphorical parables to fertilize the Earth
Wicked niggaz come, try to burglarize the turf
Scattin off soft-ass beats them niggaz rap happily
Tragically, that style, deteriorate, rapidly
Uncompleted missions, throwin your best-known compositions
You couldn't add it up, if you mastered addition

—GZA, "REUNITED," *WU-TANG FOREVER*

THE END OF THE
FIVE-YEAR PLAN

In 1997, after the release of *Wu-Tang Forever*, niggas split up from being the single unit we had been. This makes sense. The number 9-7 is a very important, pivotal one in Mathematics. And it was an important turning point in my own life. Up till then, the group was my main focus. After that I told Rae and Power, "Take Cappadonna and Deck—nurture them, make sure their shit goes proper." My brother Divine focused on Meth and Streetlife. I took Ghost and U-God. Dirty is Dirty—he's a special case. GZA kept it hooked up with Masta Killa. All this was the brand diversifying. So instead of just Nestle Quik, you've got Nestle Quik, Nestle Strawberry Quik, Diet Nestle Quik.

Divide and conquer—that was one of the main lessons I took at the very beginning of this whole Wu-Tang Clan campaign. But it's also a lesson that was used against us, because there's another side to it. What about to unite and conquer? What happens if we unite different people to conquer another? In a way, that's what happened. In a way, this plan was too good, it was too successful. It gave artists too much power. It made the industry uncomfortable. And the industry put a stop to the plan.

I've managed the business side and I've managed the creative side and, in the end, I got to say the creative side is better for you. The business is bullshit. People who are up in those offices all day, they're not doing shit. It really doesn't take all that superstructure to go ahead and make money. But you have to be focused. For me, I do my business. I got niggas helping me out, of course. But the bottom line is, my computer is right up top. It's in my head.

From the Nine
Rings of Wu-Tang
comic books

COMICS

"Egad—a maniac cutting a swath of destruction! This is a job for the Green Lantern, Thundra, or possibly . . . Ghost Rider."

"What about Superman?"

"Oh, please."

There's no place to hide once I step inside the room

Dr. Doom, prepare for the boom

Comic books are a main element of Wu-Tang because they're a main element of hip-hop in general. They always have been. Both hip-hop and comics are about styles and personalities. Comics are about special powers. And they're about teams of niggas united in one life-or-death cause. To me, hip-hop is about the same shit.

Born to European Gypsies, young Victor Von Doom witnesses his parents killed by local troops, studies his sorceress mother's book of black arts, and vows to avenge her death. He grows to amass incredible scientific and supernatural skills and wins a scholarship to Empire State University, where he meets Reed Richards and Ben Grimm, future members of the Fantastic Four. When he's expelled, he travels the world and meets some Tibetan monks who train him and craft for him a suit of body armor that also covers his face. He returns to his ancestral home, overthrows the government, crowns himself king, and begins using his nation's resources in a plot for world domination.

THE SILVER SURFER
(APPEARED 1966)

Norrin Rad is a resident of the peaceful planet Zenn-La when a godlike force known as Galactus threatens to devour his planet whole. In exchange for sparing his planet, Rad allows Galactus to make him his herald, transforming into a spectral silver figure that soars through the cosmos, finding planets for Galactus to feed upon. When he

DC Comics has the Justice League. Marvel has the Avengers, the Fantastic Four, and the X-Men. And ever since the beginning of hip-hop you see that influence, that same way of looking at the world. It goes from DJ Clark Kent up through X-Clan through Wu-Tang and beyond. Hip-hop was always a youth thing and youth read comics. The whole subculture of America—comics, martial arts movies, skateboarding—it's all part of our culture.

We all grew up collecting comics, just about everyone in the Wu-Tang Clan. I think Method Man had the most extensive collection. He had boxes and boxes of comic books he left in my house when he got kicked out. ODB's brother had a big collection. U-God, he had a lot of comics, and I did, too.

Growing up, I used to read comics like a movie. I'd make the music for it in my head, I'd see the choreography, the shots, everything—it'd take me an hour to read one, just plotting it out. I don't know if you feel comics more growing up in the projects or not, but I know you can relate to a lot of the main stories. Marvel heroes especially: they're always tragic. Something happened to these cats that made them strong but fucked them up, too. And a lot of them are about science gone wrong.

I lived in at least ten different projects and I got to see that the projects are a science project, in the same way that a prison is a science project. If you saw it, you would swear Stapleton Projects was a prison, because you got the tiers, and to go to your house, you have to walk past everybody's door on that particular floor. And you have helicopters and cameras—it's definitely jail. Everything around it is based on that same idea, that same science project. And in comics, when a science project goes wrong, it produces monsters. Or superheroes. In Marvel comics especially, every hero has some kind of fatal flaw, some tragic aspect to him. And everyone in the Wu-Tang Clan is the same way.

I was into Marvel mostly. For me, Silver Surfer was my dream hero. His powers were cosmic. He could bring the energy from the universe into his own body and transfer it back out—which is a lot like kung-fu fighting monks, using chi. I used to think of myself as the Silver Surfer. Meth, he was into Johnny Blaze, the Ghostrider. He thought Ghostrider was tougher than Silver Surfer, but I was like, "Come *on*, man."

The Silver Surfer actually appeared in a Fantastic Four issue. His story is, he got stuck on Earth trying to save it. He fell in love with Earth in a way, but his master Galactus made him stay on Earth forever. And then, Galactus went back to the Silver Surfer's planet and ate it. So the Silver Surfer was just fucked all the way around—even though he stayed righteous.

But I was also a big fan of Galactus. When I started to form the Wu-Tang Clan—around the end of my comics collection—I stopped thinking of myself as Silver Surfer and I started to think I was Galactus. Galactus, he's just bad. He's not even a villain, he's beyond that in size and scope. He's like Apocalypse in X-men. Apocalypse—basically, you don't want Apocalypse coming, because that's the end of the world. And in the Transformers, pretty much the same character is called Unicron. What they all do is consume your whole planet. Unicron, Galactus, Apocalypse—they're all Marvel characters. But they're all deeper than that, too. They're like Kronos, the father of Zeus.

As a kid, especially a single-parent kid, the one thing you really feel you need is protection. But nightmares and bad dreams? No one can protect you from those. And most kids wish they had some kind of special powers to protect themselves. It's that wish for power that makes you title yourself a hero. If you've got a lot of brothers and

comes to Earth, the surfer meets young Alicia Masters, and decides to save her planet, boldly defying the awesome Galactus. For this offense he is forever bound by a barrier around the planet—doomed to stay within Earth's sphere, soaring around and witnessing the follies of mankind. Fans have compared his plight to the biblical fall of Adam.

Yo, yo, The Riddler, funny bone tickler
Freak Caligula bigger dick sex enigma
Pistol fertilize your stigma
—RZA, "REUNITED," WU-TANG FOREVER

THE RIDDLER (APPEARED 1948)
Edward Nygma is a former childhood champion of riddles, puzzles, and brainteasers who grows up to become a criminal mastermind. Physically unremarkable, he is a match for his archenemy Batman only in his wits. He taunts Batman and the police by giving clues to his planned feats of evil in the form of dense, cryptic verbal mysteries. Although they sound like nursery rhymes or hopscotch chants, the utterances take on a powerful air of menace when known to be from the Riddler—clues to an impending campaign of terror.

IRON MAN
(APPEARED 1963)

While testing high-tech weapons in the jungles of Vietnam, millionaire inventor and arms dealer Tony Starks is nearly killed by a booby-trap explosion that embeds a piece of shrapnel in his body, working its way toward his heart. Captured and ordered to design weapons for the Vietcong, he instead constructs a metallic, transistorized suit that both acts as pacemaker and gives him superhuman powers. He defeats his captors and escapes, but is doomed to remain partially encased in metal until he dies. Starks's cover story for his alter-ego is that Iron Man is his body-guard. A wealthy patriot with a war injury, Tony Starks has been compared to John F. Kennedy.

GHOSTRIDER
(APPEARED 1972)

Raised in a carnival, young John Blaze is trained in motorcycle stunts by his foster father. When his father gets cancer, John makes a deal with the devil, Mephisto, to save him. Mephisto spares the man's life in exchange for John's soul. Mephisto ends up possessing John's body with the demonic spirit of Zarathos. Living as a carnival owner and stunt rider, John Blaze periodically turns

sisters, like I do, if something comes on TV, you had to be the first one to yell, "That's me!" And you got to be him. "I'm Steve Austin!" "I'm the Incredible Hulk!" Wrestlers, anybody that had more power than you, you wanted to be that person to help you defend your weak situation.

I see that looking at children now. I was playing with my son and he goes "shoo-shoo"—making like he's shooting powers at me. "I'm sending my powers at you!" he'd yell. And the first time he did it, I said, "You know, that really won't hurt anybody."

But the second time he did it, I didn't say that to him. Because I thought about it and realized that if you really have that will and that chi energy, and that understanding, who knows? Maybe you can fuck someone up that way. That thirty-sixth chamber in martial arts, that's the one where the fighter just forces energy at his opponent and knocks him across the room. So I don't want to take that away from a child.

It's imagination. To imagine means to image. And once you make an image, you can make flesh. It's power upon power. And it's real. That power, that force—if you let it, it can move mountains.

THE NINE RINGS OF WU-TANG
(APPEARED 2002)

The comic followed the adventures of nine Moorish warriors in feudal China, supremely gifted martial artists who are invincible as a team. The known world became their kingdom, and morality became their highest cause. With them, they would carry the ark of knowledge and the spark for future remembrance. "Ancient Wu-Tang secrets revealed in comic-book series!"

In 2002, the Wu-Tang comic-book line *The Nine Rings of Wu-Tang* replaced *X-Men* as the top comic in the country.

Wu-Tang action figures modeled after the personas from the *Nine Rings of Wu-Tang* comic books became available in 2002.

BOBBY DIGITAL

Yo, you may catch me in a pair of Polo Skipperys

Matching cap, razor blades in my gums

BOBBY!

You may catch me in yellow Havana Joe's

Goose jumper and my phaser off stun

BOBBY!

Y'all might just catch me in the park playin chess

Studyin' math, signin 7 and a sun

BOBBY!

But you won't catch me without the ratchet, in the joint

Smoked out, dead broke, or off point

BOBBY!

—RZA AS BOBBY DIGITAL,

"PROTECT YOUR NECK (THE JUMP OFF)," *THE W*

Around 1998, I became a superhero in real life. For years, I was really into heroes like Moon Knight. He had no real superpower. He was just a man. His story was that he almost died but survived and came back to life because of some kind of moon energy—it's kind of like the Crow. And also, I'm a Cancer, a moon child, so I felt like him. And the Green Hornet's another one of my favorite characters—and he's just a man, too. So I decided, "Fuck this, I'm gonna become a superhero for real."

Bobby Digital is the character I came up with for myself, my alter-ego. It's mostly a chance for me to live out some of my hip-hop past that got pushed aside by RZA. When Wu-Tang blew up, I was mostly behind the scenes, making beats, running things. So you didn't hear about the personal life experiences that molded me.

into the horrific fiery-headed being known as the Ghostrider, who tears through night streets on a flaming motorcycle, hurling balls of fire.

Alabama split, hammer slay quick
That David Banner gamma ray shit

—U-GOD "PROTECT YA NECK
(THE JUMP OFF)," *THE W*

ROBERT BRUCE BANNER (APPEARED 1962)

Nuclear physicist Robert Bruce Banner is at work on a top secret G-bomb when an accident exposes him to the bomb's deadly gamma radiation. He develops a condition wherein fits of rage transform him into a huge, green, virtually indestructible creature of limitless strength known as the Hulk. Comics have produced several incarnations of the Hulk, each one with varying levels of intelligence. The most famous version, the "Green" or "Savage" Hulk, has the mind of a child. While the Hulk's tragic dilemma, split personality, and awesome physical power might make him a natural icon for hip-hop appropriation, he's not such a popular character with MCs—possibly because his verbal dexterity is limited to statements like "Hulk smash!"

MOON KNIGHT (APPEARED 1975)

Marc Spector is a soldier of fortune working for terrorist Roald Bushman. When he is betrayed by Bushman and left for dead near an Egyptian archaeological site, Spector is found by the site workers who worship the local moon god Khonshu, also a god of vengeance. He rises from near death, declaring himself the moon's knight of vengeance, his strength intimately tied to the moon's phases. He goes on to avenge himself. Like the Shadow and the Green Hornet, the Moon Knight isn't a supernaturally powerful being, but a mortal whose allies and operatives help him achieve victory. He works under several different identities that allow him to move through society undetected. One is Steven Grant, a playboy millionaire whose base of operations is the Grant Mansion, in Long Island. Another is Jake Lockley, a cabdriver who knows every street in Manhattan.

So I did the album *Bobby Digital in Stereo* and the film *Bobby Digital*. The film introduces you to Bobby in the '80s, when he's just a regular nigga with no knowedge—he's a B-boy, into gangs, with the long '80s braids. He finally gets tired of seeing niggas shoot at each other. So he's on some "Put away your guns! Let's fight with our hands!" trip. But there's some crooked police won't let the static die because there's too much money in drugs and guns in the ghetto and they force Bobby underground.

Underground, he has a laboratory where he makes this serum called the "honey serum," which he uses to make honey-dipped blunts. And when he hits one, it transforms him, opens up his consciousness. Throughout the movie you see him keep returning to the laboratory, trying to make a better formula each time.

Then there's a twelve-year gap and he comes back in the '90s as a superhero. He has transformed himself. He has acquired a lot of wealth and he wears a mask, like Green Lantern. He discovers a digital signal that can exist inside a man, so he hooks up some computers in the lab, and mixes chemicals to get this signal into physical form. And eventually the lab explodes, but he's transformed to the point that he can travel through digital signals.

In the movie, he's going through the ghetto, noticing that there's a digital revolution going on in the world around, but the ghetto's stuck in analog. They don't have Internet access, don't have digital phones. So his mission is to implant a little signal into man, so they won't have to rely on anything else for entertainment or to get information. So he puts the digital signal into a bullet. Instead of shooting you and killing you, this bullet awakens you. It digitizes you.

When you become digital, you become digits—pure Mathematics. So, to be digital means to see things clearly, for what they are and not what they appear to be. For Bobby Digital, man is like an antenna; and we walk on too much concrete to stay grounded. So this breaks our frequency. This is also a lot like some understandings of chi, the way some kung fu teaches you to stay grounded for more power.

So Bobby Digital is about what molded me: comic books, video games, the arcade scene, breakdancing, hip-hop clothes, MCing, DJing, human beatboxing, graffiti plus Mathematics and the gods. That's hip-hop to me.

Eventually, though, I took it to the final level. Even outside making music and films, I was on it. I decided to become Bobby Digital for real. I had the car and I had the suit. I was getting ready to go out at nighttime and right some wrongs. That was my plan—like on some Green Hornet shit. I had this suit built for me that's literally invulnerable to AK fire. The car was a black Suburban that I had made bulletproof and bombproof up to government-security-level standards. I called it the Black Tank. I still have it—it stays at the Bat Cave. I even had a good butler almost ready to go. He was going to be like my Kato, but he wasn't old enough yet. I was really on a mission, I really felt compelled. I spent hundreds of thousands of dollars. To get Bobby Digital up and online. To keep it real. That's how seriously I took it.

**VOLTRON
(APPEARED 1984)**

Five of the brightest, toughest graduates of the Space Academy, the quintet of Voltron Force are trapped on Planet Doom and used as slave gladiators before they escape to travel to Planet Arus and resurrect the mightiest robot in the galaxy, Voltron, Defender of the Universe. Keith, an expert swordsman, is commander of the team and pilots the Black Lion, which forms Voltron's head and torso. Lance, his second, pilots the Red Lion, Voltron's sword-wielding right arm. Martial arts expert Pidge pilots the Green Lion, Voltron's left arm. Allura pilots the Blue Lion, the right leg, and the volatile Hunk pilots the Yellow Lion, Voltron's left leg.

CHESS

Chess is . . .

. . . everything: art, science, and sport.

— ANATOLY KARPOV

. . . a black and white jungle.

— GARRY KASPAROV

. . . . like a swordfight. You must think first, before you move.

— INTRO SAMPLE,
"THE MYSTERY OF CHESSBOXIN',"
ENTER THE WU-TANG: 36 CHAMBERS

Chess is a very important element of Wu-Tang. It's an important element of life. It teaches you how to exist in the world. It teaches you to think multiple moves ahead, to strategize. It teaches you how to attack, how to defend.

It's one game niggas like to play just to test the mind—it's very relaxing and a good way to release stress. To me that's a perfect afternoon: playing chess all day, watching kung-fu movies, smoking a few blunts, and making a beat—I'm in heaven.

But chess also gets very, very serious. You talk with any true player, he takes it like a life-or-death experience.

I learned chess when I was eleven years old, from a girl. The same girl who took my virginity, she also taught me how to play chess. I started to love the game as a game—it's fun, it's a thinking game. When I was growing up, I used to go to Wall Street and hang at the park and play the old men, get whipped, start playing for money. But as I got older, I realized that chess was more than a game.

It's a strategic game that helps to calculate life, business, power moves. A good chess player can think three to four moves ahead. If you can do that, you can really manipulate a situation so that you're winning.

I was one of the original players in the group and at first I was the best. The only ones playing were me and GZA and Killa. I was the man for a few years. Then GZA became the man, then Killa became the man. But now it goes around. And as time went on, other Clan members became interested by watching us doing it so much. And so Deck picked it up, U-God got into it. But still, now, I play my best games with GZA and Killa.

If it's quiet and just me and you, one on one, that's when you know: If you beat me that day, you beat me. That's very rare.

. . . in its essence a game, in its form an art, and in its execution a science.

—BARON TASSILO VON HEYDERBRAND

. . . a kind of mental alcohol . . . unless a man has supreme self-control. It is better that he should not learn to play [it].

—HENRY BLACKBURNE

. . . a work of art between minds, which need to balance two sometimes disparate goals—to win, and to produce beauty.

—VASILY SMYSLOV

Another reason chess is part of the Wu-Tang essence is because it's a game of war—it's about a battle. And Wu-Tang was formed in battles, from challenging each other. In MCing, the Wu-Tang Clan was always powerful because we were challenging each other all the time. At any moment, anybody in the crew could be the best MC that day.

I remember reading about Stanley Kubrick keeping a chess set on every film set—to keep his mind focused, but also to see if anyone would ever want to challenge him. That was his way of letting everybody know that he was the one in charge. It was like hustling in the park. But he would just keep it around so if you ever had any doubt who the man is, step to the board.

We look at chess in terms of the group. That's why we made the video "Chessboxing." In that video GZA and I were the captains, and everyone else was pieces. Somebody was a bishop, somebody was a rook. In chess,

My growth in chess shows lyrically. When I did *Words from Genius,* I didn't say anything about chess. I wasn't playing so much. I did *Liquid Swords,* and I speak about chess numerous times. One song I say, "He got swung on, his lungs were torn/the kingpin just castled a rook and lost a pawn." It's not like it's coincidental. It's something that's a part of us, of what we do. Instead of running around saying, "I rhyme about what I live, it's all real," it'll show in your words. You don't have to say it.

It's like RZA, he mentions something about chess, he says something about "My thoughts be sneaky like a crook from Brooklyn/ When he ain't lookin I take the queen with the rook and . . . " It's part of it. Chess just opens up and unlocks many different doors. It's a part of what we do.

there's only three characters—bishop, knight, and rook—and you got two of each. Then you got the queen, king, and pawns. But we never point out who's who. You might hear Raekwon say in a rap, "I'm a bishop," or "I'm a castle." But they change it up. And, you can't really say Ol' Dirty Bastard is a rook or a king or a bishop—he's in a class by himself.

At parties chess was considered nerdy at one point. Now it's considered cool. Other rappers play it, lots of brothers are into it. You'll hear it, a chess game sound like a game of street basketball. The other day, when GZA was playing Melquan, when he took his queen he said, "Hey, your bitch chose me"—that is some pimp shit. That's just how we flip it.

> . . . a game in which are revealed your intellect, character, will.
>
> —BORIS SPASSKY

> . . . a universal game that cuts across all of those artificial boundaries we set up to segregate ourselves from our fellow human beings.
>
> —STEVE LOPEZ

> . . . an art appearing in the form of a game.
>
> —A SOVIET ENCYCLOPEDIA

MATHEMATICS OF CHESS

I look at chess in a metaphysical way. There are sixty-four squares on the board. Throughout Mathematics and throughout history, sixty-four is a deep number. The sixty-four squares are in eight columns, which relates to the eight points of the sun. And 1964 was the year when the Father first came and brought the lessons. Plus, sixty-four squares is similar to the *I Ching,* which has sixty-four hexagrams total, and the *I Ching* is how to calculate the universe. Sixty-four is also a very creative number. When the sperm meets the egg and they have meiosis, it splits into sixty-four separate cells–two to four, four to eight, then eight to sixty-four. That's one life cell. Sixty-four is the basic number of creation.

People say, "Chess is life," and that's real. It really is about life at the most basic level. That's why I have a rap that says, "Sixty-four lines up into eight columns, we meditate, we calculate life's problems." Life has a lot to do with the sixty-four squares. It's black and white, yin and yang. White always goes first–you don't have to work too hard to connect that to human history: Whites have been antagonistic by nature; Africans are more humble by nature.

Chess also teaches you not to respect all your men, all your soldiers by the same criteria, especially the ones that aren't such obvious players. Power comes from suprising places. The knight, for example, isn't the most obvious power piece, but it is the most Mathematical. It moves in a right angle of two steps up and one left. It's also close to God because its course traces a number seven on the board. You have to be super careful around the knight. To me the knight and the rook are the two most dangerous men on the board. If I have my knights and my rooks, I'm still a very formidable foe. If you take my queen, I'm still a come at you. And the queen can do every other pieces's move, but she can't do the knight's.

There are eight pawns, but the pawn is the only piece on the board that has the power to be anything at all. In all reality, whether it's the knight, the rook, or the queen, they're all on a mission to protect the king. A lot of people say that the most powerful piece on the board is the queen, but it's really the king who's the most powerful. You can kill the queen and the game still goes on.

THE WU-TANG SACRIFICE

There's one move I used to do a lot. It was a sacrifice technique I used to use that won a lot of games in the early days.

Basically, it's when your knight hits the king's pawn. At C2, shall we say. In the first five moves on the game. So the king's knight—say black knight, because I'm working from the black side—hits the king's pawn at F2. Usually, your opponent will kill your knight. He'll take it with his king—which is the only piece he can take it with. So that's a pretty serious loss early in the game: your knight. But it draws the king out of a castling position. I used to win a lot of games like that. Once the king is out of a castling position, I had a certain attack designed that was coming down on you after that. But basically the idea is this: Sacrifice for a position. You let that knight go to lure that king out to where he can't castle, because it's harder to defeat the castle defense.

That particular move is an opening move. I'd probably use that on somebody with a low chess rating. It's more a beginning phase, but people figure it out. I first developed that idea back in '94. It's still a good one to bring out early, when you're just trying to test someone's skills.

Popa Wu says that a lot of players protect their queen at all costs. Which is also like life—a man loses his woman, he flips out, acts stupid. So a lot of players, they tend to identify themselves with the king. But if you're a master player you realize that you're not the king either. You're actually playing God. That's how I see it anyway. You're not any piece on the board. You're all the pieces. If the king dies, you don't die. So in a way what that should teach you is, don't take it so serious.

. . . 99 percent tactics.

—RICHARD TEICHMANN

. . . 99 percent calculation.

—ANDREW SOLTIS

. . . ruthless: you've got to be prepared to kill people.

—NIGEL SHORT

Chess is a martial art. So in that way, it's about the flow of chi, the ebbing and flowing of universal energies. Because when you got a good streak in chess, you probably got a good streak in everything you're doing. You're just pushing energy forth. When I'm feeling really really good, and my confidence is really up, you're not going to beat me in the game of chess. Or in anything. That's why it's my season, my moment. Chess is a good measurement. When I'm on a streak, I'm on a streak in everything. Even in my own crew, there are days when you know—"Man, I ain't fucking with him today. He'll whip me three games in a row."

But it can keep you a humble warrior, too. It teaches you to stay on point no matter what. You never know if you're truly skilled in chess because I could come across a seven-year-old kid that could beat me because he has the wits and foresight. I've won a lot of games in my life, but I lost a few, too, and had a few crushing defeats. One kid caught me on tour. It was after my show and he caught me off guard. I did one of my amateur moves—a move that, you know, "He fall for this one, maybe you know you be aight." It was a sacrifice move. But he was too good for that. He came and defeated me. At the end, I had to respect him. He was super good—*computer* good.

Chess also taught me never to give up. That's one of my main tactics: Never count me out. It's the same with the greatest players. They play right up to that last move, and they never give up. I've won many victories just when you thought I was about to lose.

ORGANIZED CRIME

At the time we were coming up, most of us were outlaws, for real. We had our own experiences in the street game, especially Ghost and Rae. But also, at that time, Staten Island was one of the main homes to the Gambino crime family. Castellano was the boss before Gotti, he lived on Staten Island, and his kids went to school there. We'd see him there, we'd come across kids from his family.

Even after the Wu-Tang Clan became famous, I still knew a few guys I had met from that family, and I met a few new ones. I guess they came by to meet us out of respect. So we took on that name. It just seemed to flow.

Raekwon brought the whole idea of the Wu Gambinos to the forefront during the *Cuban Linx* album, but it was always there, in the background.

When Raekwon came with *Cuban Linx,* he started everyone in hip-hop fiending for that mafia shit. It was an explosion. The album was a lot like the crime movies in the way it mixed parables and drama and fantasy with real-life stories from Rae and Ghost's time in the street game. Rae and Ghost—those two are the biggest criminologists in Wu-Tang. They know it—for real—but they're amazing MCs and amazing storytellers. Rae had every MC who was on that album take a new name for it, starting with him, Lex Diamonds. You can't tell where one stops and the other begins. That's kind of the beauty of it.

Some kinds of movies you love because they're just great movies. Other movies hit you deeper. You love them because they show you something you recognize from life, from the shit you see every day. All of us, together and separately, we were fans not just of *The Godfather* trilogy, *Goodfellas,* and *Scarface,* but all the crime movies— *Mob Wars, Cotton Club, Gang Wars, Once Upon a Time in America, Billy Bathgate* to way before that. Plus, there's all the Chinese crime movies—John Woo joints and all those before him. Basically, if it's a crime movie, a nigga wants to see it.

It's not that they're all necessarily great movies, but they reflect what we see around us in a way you don't see in other films. Some films hold that essence, they dramatize realities, shit that you see played out in the street game every day.

It was a validation of everything I believed in. It was basically the way I saw the life.

—SALVATORE "SAMMY THE BULL" GRAVANO,
ON *THE GODFATHER* (YEARS AFTER SEEING THE FILM,
GRAVANO WAS INDUCTED INTO THE GAMBINO FAMILY FOR REAL)

The Godfather and *Scarface*, in particular, are very serious. They're almost biblical, in terms of their importance in life. I studied *The Godfather* over and over and over while making the Wu-Tang Clan.

If you look at Vito Corleone, he was a great godfather because he was ruthless and he was fair. And when he was ruthless, his ruthlessness was part of his fairness. I may have caught that lesson first in the movie, but believe me, I saw it over and over and over again in real life. I wanted to be Vito Corleone and I modeled myself after him in a lot of ways.

When I went in to shop the Wu-Tang Clan to labels, I was going in to make them an offer they couldn't refuse. It wasn't that they'd get whacked if they turned me down. It was that I was too strong, had too much intention. I was too certain to be refused. I was sure about what I was doing. I knew we were invincible as MCs and that the plan would work.

Vito Corleone

Also, Vito Corleone had this cool to him, he was logical. He kept his priorities straight. Even when they killed his son, he didn't destroy the whole business that he made. When they killed Sonny, he didn't get emotional and go kill everybody on some wild maniac shit. He kept his business in hand and really planned and let his family live on. And eventually, his family became worth six hundred million dollars— legally. You see that in *Godfather III*. That's very inspirational, the whole story, and I knew I wanted that for my family, and for the Wu-Tang Clan.

Scarface, that was about doing anything necessary to make it to the top. *Scarface* is every hip-hop nigga's dream, becoming a millionaire by living the street life. But the film also shows you a very important lesson about the game of life. Scarface, Tony Montana, made one basic error.

His error was not seeing that a moral-less man cannot choose the time in life to *get* morals. In the movie, Tony Montana caught morality at the wrong time. He caught morality over the women and children he didn't want to blow up. So he fucked up his man for that. He blew it. You can't suddenly get morals—that will kill you. It even says that in the Holy Koran, when the people go to hell, they called out to the saved people to help them. And Abraham wanted to help them, but God didn't. So basically, you might as well enjoy it because you're not getting out of it.

Tony Montana might as well have blown up that car, killed those women and children, and stayed loyal to his team. Because he was gone already, already in hell. He had a limitation to his wickedness—he wouldn't kill any children. But that limitation was artifical, it was arbitrary on his part. And it was the end of him. The point is, you better go all the way. You can't serve two masters. You better serve God or serve the devil.

I control twenty-six thousand men. Except for dope, we operate in every aspect of organized crime. And if there's one thing I'm sure of, it's that drugs destroy your mind and destroy your home. In the end, it will only lead our country into ruin.

—FROM 1995 JAPANESE CRIME FILM *CRYING FREEMAN*, SAMPLED IN INTRO TO GHOSTFACE KILLAH'S "FISH"

In a way, we took some of the structure of the Wu-Tang from a mob chain of command. They've usually got a don, who's the boss, and a consigliere, and then they got an underboss and capos, who are generals to the street soldiers. They all answer to the underboss.

The thing about Wu-Tang, it isn't just me and eight lackeys, it's nine generals. Each one of the main generals has other niggas they control. So when we came together it was like everybody held up a pillar.

Wu-Tang started out as a dictatorship. Then it went to something like a democracy. That's when everyone became generals, with a lot of guys under them. They can all function independently, although they're organized under one umbrella, one family.

In the end, the most important value you take away from crime movies and from mafia tales is loyalty. You gotta have your team. The idea of family, the code of honor, we live by that. Even to this day, we live by that. This is why when someone gets on the radio and says something, everybody gets involved, everybody's gotta check in.

Everybody called me, for instance, when U-God was on the radio saying some angry things. Basically people called asking me how I felt. If I would've felt funny about it, it would've been something. But I didn't. I didn't want to make it serious.

When Dirty signed to Roc-A-Fella, I got e-mails calling him Fredo. Fans were saying that he turned on us. But I didn't necessarily see it that way. I look back to *The Godfather*. Didn't Luca Brasi go and join that other family for a while? He had his reasons. You learn more, you grow. You can't always worry about how it looks to outsiders.

We've all got serious history together, we've been around each other for years and we've got a code of honor. And that's what following the mafia instilled in us. We're family, and we're not gonna let each other destroy that. Before I destroy Wu-Tang, I'm going to go live on a mountain. If I realize that I'm the problem, then I need to handle it.

That one critical scene in *The Godfather,* when the guy goes in the tub and cuts his own wrists—that was a big scene to us. If you want to go out, that's the way. He showed his loyalty to the cause and to his own family.

From Masta Killa's
video collection

CINEMA

Obviously, all of the Wu-Tang Clan is heavy into movies. You hear it everywhere, from the kung-fu samples, to the John Woo references, to the mob flicks—it's everywhere, it's part of our lives. But to me, hip-hop *is* moviemaking. When you write a song, you tell a story and you take on a persona, an attitude. It could be you, it could be based on you, or it could be not you at all. But you take it on, that's part of the process.

You take Method Man as an example. He made that song, but he *became* Method Man. He became that character. Around 1991 or 1992. I said, "Your name is Method Man. You are *the* Method Man now." Then we made a song.

You see him now—he plays other roles and does other characters, in films, on TV, wherever. But behind those characters is the first character that he really and truly became, which was Method Man.

My idea from the beginning was to make each of the albums a little movie. Look at the first title: *Enter the Wu-Tang: 36 Chambers.* You read that, it's like, "What is that all about?" It doesn't explain itself to you like a lot of albums do. You come in cold, the same way you might wander into a movie theater on Forty-Second Street late some night.

Then you hear, "*The Shaolin and the Wu-Tang . . . could be dangerous.*" Then it's like, "Oh *shit!*" You know you're going to go through this whole episode of music and drama—someone's getting shot, someone's getting flipped, someone's fighting—and you don't even know where you're at.

I used to make certain albums hoping they'd come out in winter—like *36 Chambers* or *Liquid Swords.* The only album I wanted to come out in the summer was *Cuban Linx.* It's like directing, and I directed those first ones to have a wintertime vibe. It's more inside-your-car, more intimate with the music. Whereas in the summer, it's more out in the world with it. So with *Cuban Linx* it's more of an out-in-the-world type of album. *Liquid Swords, 36 Chambers*—those are wintertime, up-in-your-face joints. You really feel it. Songs like "Cold World" with the wind blowing, I want people to be in their cars, just . . . shivering.

New York is a tough place in the winter. Everybody's got big jackets, you don't know what kind of gun they're carrying underneath. Especially in those days, it was just crazy. That's how it is with me making music. I'm creating a whole atmosphere, a whole world.

Synesthesia: A condition in which the normally separate senses are not separate. Sight may mingle with sound, taste with touch, etc. The senses are cross-wired. For example, when a digit-color synesthete sees or just thinks of a number, the number appears with a color film over it. A given number's color never changes; it appears every time with the number. Synesthesia can take many forms. A synesthete may sense the taste of chicken as a pointed object. Other synesthetes hear colors. Still others may have several senses cross-wired.

—WEBSTER'S NEW WORLD MEDICAL DICTIONARY

CINEMATIC SPARKS

I can still remember the first four movies I ever saw, in order. It went *Tom Sawyer,* then *Rocky,* then *Star Wars,* then *The Swarm.* Straight up, that was it. You can see the influence of those first movies throughout the Wu-Tang and my career. The *Star Wars* and *Rocky* movies you can definitely hear in the music.

Star Wars had a super impact on me. Of course it has a super impact on a whole generation. To me, *Star Wars* is actually based on the myths of the Teutonic knights, and there's some old Kurosawa influence in there—like *Seven Samurai* and *The Hidden Fortress.* But I didn't look at it like that until later. At the time, it was just a fascination with the story and the drama.

As far as the impact of *The Swarm,* you saw that with the Wu-Tang idea of killer bees. The idea of the Wu-Tang killer bees came early, even before we did "Clan in da Front"—"Wu-Tang killa bees—we on a swarm." *The Swarm* was one of my first movies, but part of the song was inspired by the news at the time.

Everyone had been talking about this lethal force of killer bees were supposed to hit America. There was some panic about it and all sorts of stories in the papers and on the news about them. But those killer bees from Africa, they never hit. Instead, we hit. *We* were the killer bees.

JOHN WOO

With John Woo, I've just had the privilege to get a lot of advice from him. First of all, studying all his movies gave me a lot of insight into storytelling, the flow of cutting, the ways to shoot. And then, later, meeting him personally, I was able to ask him why he shot this scene this way, why he wrote the story that way, and so on. He gave me a lot of in-depth insight into his movies.

When he told me about *Bullet in the Head*—one of his first movies—why he wrote it, how he wrote it, how it related to his life, I realized he had a similar life to mine as far as growing up in poverty, coming up in this cultural revolution, and the reformation that they had back then. And I could reflect that on growing up in my neighborhood, with the police against you and always feeling trapped.

There's so much he taught me, but I'll just share one simple kind of rule. It's almost like a koan. He taught me that the director has to have the mind of an editor. And you must find an editor that has the mind of a director. I'll just leave it there.

JARMUSCH

Ghost Dog. Power, equality.

—RZA, AS "SAMURAI IN CAMOUFLAGE," GREETING FOREST
WHITAKER'S GHOST DOG ON THE STREET

I met Jim Jarmusch through a friend of mine, a rapper named Dreddy Kruger. Around the time I did the Bobby Digital album, Dreddy came to my office with Jim and Jim said he wanted me to do the music for his movie. I think he chose me because of the martial arts aspect of the Wu-Tang Clan and his understanding of the code we live by—the brotherhood and loyalty. Because that's really what *Ghost Dog* was about.

Jim, me, and Forest Whitaker met. Jim said he'd write the script, he told Forest to practice for the part, and I'd go work on the music. It was informal, intuitive. In a way, it was like doing a hip-hop record.

When he asked me to do *Coffee and Cigarettes*, I thought he wanted me to do the music, but he said he wrote a part for me. So GZA and I ended up acting in a scene with Bill Murray. That one, I didn't see coming.

TARANTINO

I met Quentin on a panel promoting the Hong Kong action movie *Iron Monkey*. I knew that he liked blaxploitation movies from having seen *Jackie Brown,* but I didn't know he was into kung-fu flicks. But at that panel, we started talking kung-fu flicks, and next thing you know we're battling with it, trying to pull out titles the other one didn't know.

Then he told me he was working on *Kill Bill*, and that he'd like me to be involved. I think he'd just had one of those Wu-Tang weeks, when he was playing Wu every day. It was just natural. I'm known as a resurrector and so is Quentin, in his field. We're both known for bringing people back to life.

HIP-HOP SCORING

I always try to make my music visual, to make you see pictures, and soundtracks let me explore that even more. Also, when you're making a hip-hop record, you're usually dealing with a loop that's either two or four bars long. But with a soundtrack, you can stretch it out. In some of my film work, I'll go twelve or sixteen bars before I repeat the first note. Most hip-hop producers don't ever get to do that.

I'm an action film lover, and to me, most action films either don't have good music or they don't cut it right. It doesn't really match the scene. You'll have some techno going on, and it's not moving with the movement of the film or the action, especially American-made martial arts movies. If you ever watch *The Black Mask,* with Jet Li, the action is good, but the music makes the action seem corny. In the old kung-fu movies, the action can be mediocre, but the music gets you excited. It gets you hyped up. It's like there are certain types of music that Superman just can't fly to. You need the right music to get it popping.

Since I started composing film scores, I got into studying music more, the theory of it, the instrumentation. In between Wu-Tang albums, I took the time to become a trained musician. I always felt that my music was cinematic anyway. I was probably one of the first people to sample Hollywood theme music and mix it into hip-hop—at least in the way I did it, to the extent that I really tried to fuse them on this molecular level.

I know that Hollywood has been using hip-hop producers to do their film music more and more recently, and in a lot of cases that's just a fad. But hip-hop itself was called a fad for a long time. Hip-hop scoring is not going to disappear if a few studio executives give up on it.

I have the knowledge of the theory of music, I can play the things myself, or I can pull it out of my collection and play the right thing at the right time. *Kill Bill: Vol. 1* was more of a hip-hop DJ score, because it was what we call a "pull-out" soundtrack—meaning you just pull things out of your collection that work. Quentin had his turntable there—all types of vinyl—I had the MPC 4000 sampler, plus a Fantom keyboard because I like to play some things naturally. That's a lot of what me and Quentin did, mixed with more traditional composing.

But by the time I scored *Soul Plane,* it was actually an orchestra playing my music.

RZA BEHIND THE CAMERA

I'm definitely looking forward to doing something serious in Hollywood, like directing a major motion picture. I'd show some of the urban culture, from a real person who lived it. Seeing how much time and money people in Hollywood waste making movies, I know I could do the whole film—and it'd be a good film—for what they'd budget for just the music. In hip-hop, I learned to work fast and efficiently.

I've researched Hollywood for a while. I know that Quincy Jones started off as a big-band musician and a composer and producer and he scored movies and TV shows and eventually started producing TV shows. So I'm a mission like that, like him and Bill Cosby.

I've directed and codirected Wu-Tang videos, Gravediggaz videos, and some straight-up films. In 1998, we did the film *Wu-Tang,* which is kind of like a home movie of the group itself. I acted in and directed the Bobby Digital film, and directed the short film *Domestic Violence,* which is the first release by Wu-Tang Filmz. There's also our kung-fu flick, *The Z Chronicles,* which stars Sifu Shi Yan-Ming as the Abbot. He does some fight sequences and I become the Abbot in the middle of the movie.

In film, I've already had some of the best mentors: John Woo, Jim Jarmusch, and Quentin Tarantino. When I worked with Quentin, I was working on *The Z Chronicles.* And I asked him if I could use the opportunity to get mentored by him. That's the best way to learn something. Quentin would let me look though the lens, see how he'd be setting up shots, show me how they did different camera moves in '70s kung-fu films. It's how Thomas Jefferson learned different skills— he apprenticed at them.

I feel that no matter how big the Wu-Tang Clan gets we're still underground in spirit. And I'd want any films I did to be the same way. I like low-budget films a lot. And making them you have more creative control. If I don't get that, I'm not doing it. In some ways, I feel I've already directed, produced, and acted in some of the hardest, illest movies out there. It's just that they're on wax.

WU-TANG MOVIE STARS

ACTING ROLES BY THE NINE GENERALS

RZA
Breaking the Rules (2005) (filming)
Coffee and Cigarettes (2004) . . . . Himself
Scary Movie 3 (2003) . . . . Himself
Ghost Dog: The Way of the Samurai (1999) . . . . Samurai in Camouflage
Wu-Tang (1998) . . . . Himself
Rhyme & Reason (1997) . . . . Himself

NOTABLE TV GUEST APPEARANCES
America's Next Top Model (2003) . . . . Himself ("The Girl Who Is Dripping with Hypocrisy") February 24, 2004
Chappelle's Show (2004) . . . . Himself ("The Racial Draft"—episode #201) January 21, 2004
Chappelle's Show (2003) . . . . Himself ("Wu-Tang Financial"—episode #107) March 5, 2003
Upright Citizens Brigade (1999) . . . . Himself (as Bobby Digital) ("Bomb Squad") June 21, 1999
The Larry Sanders Show (1998) . . . . Himself ("Adolf Hankler"— episode #84) April 19, 1998

GZA

Coffee and Cigarettes (2003) . . . Himself
Wu-Tang (1998) . . . Himself

NOTABLE TV GUEST APPEARANCES

Chappelle's Show (2004) . . . . Himself ("The Racial Draft"—episode #201) January 21, 2004
Chappelle's Show (2003) . . . . Musical Guest (episode #10) March 26, 2003
Chappelle's Show (2003) . . . . Himself ("Wu-Tang Financial"—episode #107) March 5, 2003

Ol' Dirty Bastard

Wu-Tang (1998) . . . Himself

NOTABLE TV GUEST APPEARANCES

America's Next Top Model (2003) . . . . Himself: ("The Girl Who Is Dripping with Hypocrisy") February 24, 2004
MTV Video Music Awards 2003 (2003) . . . . Himself (as Dirt McGirt)

Method Man

Method & Red (2004) TV Series . . . . Method Man
Soul Plane (2004) . . . . Muggsy
Garden State (2004) . . . . Diego
My Baby's Daddy (2004) . . . . No Good
Def Jam: Fight for NY (2004) (Videogame)
Scarface: Origins of a Hip Hop Classic (2003) (Video) . . . . Himself
Def Jam Vendetta (2003) (Videogame) . . . . Himself
Scary Movie 3 (2003) . . . . Himself
The Wire (2003) TV Series . . . . Melving "Cheese" Flagstaff
Stung (2002) TV Series . . . . Host
Oz (2001) TV Series . . . . #010251 Carlton "Tug" Daniels
How High (2001) . . . . Silas P. Silas
Whasango (2001) . . . . Mr. Ma (MTV English Dub)
. . . aka *Hwasan Highschool* (2001) (literal English title)
. . . aka *Volcano High* (2001)
Boricua's Bond (2000)
P.I.G.S. (1999) . . . . Pan-handling Nun
Black and White (1999) . . . . Himself
Wu-Tang (1998) . . . . Himself
Belly (1998) . . . . Shameek
Cop Land (1997) . . . . Shondel
One Eight Seven (1997) . . . . Dennis Broadway
Rhyme & Reason (1996) . . . . Himself

Great White Hype (1996) . . . . Himself
The Show (1995) . . . . Himself
NOTABLE TV GUEST APPEARANCES
Boston Public (2003) . . . . Flash Master K ("Chapter Sixty-five") May 5, 2003
The Twilight Zone (2003) . . . . Kneigh ("The Path") January 8, 2003
MTV Video Music Awards 2003 (2003) . . . . Himself
Third Watch (2002) . . . . C-Note ("Superheroes: Part 1") February 25, 2002
Behind the Music . . . . Himself ("Notorious B.I.G.") July 8, 2003
Space Ghost Coast to Coast (1996) . . . . Himself ("Surprise") June 19, 1996

Ghostface Killah

Def Jam Fight for NY (2004) (Videogame) . . . . Himself
Scarface: Origins of a Hip Hop Classic (2003) (Video) . . . . Himself
Def Jam Vendetta (2003) (Videogame) . . . . Himself
Big Wigs (2002) (Video) . . . . Himself
Black and White (1999) . . . . Himself
Wu-Tang (1998) . . . . Himself

Raekwon

Coalition (2004) (post-production) . . . . Akey
Scary Movie 3 (2003) . . . . Himself
Kingpin (2003) TV Mini-series . . . . Himself
Scarface: Origins of a Hip Hop Classic (2003) (Video) . . . . Himself
Black and White (1999) . . . . Cigar
Wu-Tang (1998) . . . . Himself
Rhyme & Reason (1996) . . . . Himself

Inspectah Deck

Black and White (1999) . . . . Himself
Wu-Tang (1998) . . . . Himself

U-God

Scary Movie 3 (2003) . . . . Himself
Wu-Tang (1998) . . . . Himself

Masta Killa

Black and White (1999) . . . . Himself
Wu-Tang (1998) . . . . Himself

CHEMISTRY

All the vegetable sedatives and narcotics, all the euphorics that grow on trees, the hallucinogens that ripen in berries or can be squeezed from roots—all, without exception, have been known and systematically used by human beings from time immemorial.

—ALDOUS HUXLEY

I think marijuana is just nature's way of sayin' "Hi."

—METHOD MAN

I want to set this part off by saying I don't advocate the use of illegal drugs and the Wu-Tang don't either. No one sees the misery and problems drugs can cause better than someone who grows up how we did where we did.

But the fact is, drugs are chemicals. They're just compounds of elements. You can't say they're all bad or they're all good. They're all part of the same physical universe that you have to balance to stay healthy and righteous.

I study chi gong, which teaches you how to move and balance chi inside you. Part of that is teaching about herbs and medicines the Chinese have been using for centuries to help balance that chi. Herbologists or acupuncturists will prescribe certain herbs based on your chi balance. Once you study that, you realize you can't judge substances so quickly. You have to look at it in a context.

Everything is broken down to a molecular level in the body. Every time we eat, our body is constantly regenerating. I don't think we even know the extent of our power to regenerate. The best medicine, the best drug you can take, is one well-balanced meal a day with water. That's the best herbal or medicinal treatment you can do.

When people want to take boosts, they might take some ginseng. But then if you got a cold, it's bad for you. You have to be aware of every variable really, break it down to the essence and to where you're at.

My dream after all this is to become a doctor or a scientist of some kind. But that's how I feel I am already. Believe me, I've witnessed and participated in a whole lot of experiments.

$C_{21}H_{30}O_2$
Tetrahydrocannabinol (THC)

AKA: chronic, herbalz, buds, meth, tical, methtical, indo, hydro, that shit

---

Psychoactive substance found in cannabis, a tall, leafy plant with three species (*Cannabis sativa, Cannabis indica,* and *Cannabis ruderalis*), THC has been used in various parts of the world for thousands of years. The reported effects of THC include relaxation, euphoria, altered space-time perception, enhancement of visual, auditory, and olfactory senses, disorientation, hilarity, excitability, nausea, anxiety, redness of the eyes, increased appetite, and paranoia.

I think each member definitely had a different substance or substances that they got heavy into. And we've gone through different phases as a group.

But for the whole Wu history, the one thing that goes way back to the beginning is weed. And I got to say it's also the best thing, at least for us. The best thing for making music has really been some good weed.

The vibe in *36 Chambers* was definitely a lot of weed. But in a way, it was latent. The vibe there in the making of that record was due to a lot of years of smoking and drinking that just built up and came out.

I don't mean to advocate it, I'm not advising it, but I know that for us, making music, you got to have some good weed in the spot. I think weed has been involved in at least 85 percent of all our music.

$C_{17}H_{21}NO_4$
Cocaine Hydrochloride

AKA: coke, blow, snow, flake, girl, white, uptown

Both a central nervous system stimulant and an anesthetic, cocaine was first extracted from coca leaves and used medically in the 1800s, although evidence of its use in the raw form goes back to 3000 B.C.

I didn't know it at the time, but cocaine influenced a lot of the best rapping on *36 Chambers*. Maybe you can hear it?

One of the most hectic times in Wu-Tang history was when motherfuckers was getting stained. You know they rap that line, "We getting stained with the hardware"? Stained—that's taking angel dust.

Digi is another word for it. You say, "Yo, let me get some digi." It's dust mixed with weed. You take the blunt and you pour PCP in it when you roll it.

Then . . . you're *gone*. But you're also *there*. It's hard to explain. You go places—you're on earth and space at the same time. You just turn into a superhero. As far as making music, you're staying up all night, rocking. At least you feel that way at the time.

PCP is a crystallized drug. But even if you're smoking weed, the molecular structure of it, mixing with your blood, hits your brain and makes your brain produce a pulse that's responding to that. It has a destiny encoded in that. And that destiny can be fucked up.

I'd say we all experimented with a lot of drugs. But hip-hop, this is a mental game. You got to see your way through it.

You're dealing with energies and chemicals to project a certain type of frequencies out of the mouth. Like cocaine and heroin—I know why rappers use cocaine and heroin, because it puts them in a trance state and they write these ill songs. Acid, ecstasy—it puts you into that state of trance to where you feel that's *you*. Coke—it makes motherfuckers hype. Weed—it's like a down, it makes you think like a fucking Socrates, makes you think real deep. Mushrooms do the same shit, too.

But all that shit all corresponds together. Sex, drugs, rock and roll, money, alcohol—all that shit is a part of that fucking whirlpool of creativity, especially in hip-hop. It's funny, man. But in the midst of that, motherfuckers get hooked. You become an addict.

$C_{20}H_{25}N_{30}$
Lysergic Acid Diethylamide

AKA: LSD, acid, tabs, doses, blotter, hits, Bart Simpsons, windowpane

Discovered in Switzerland's Sandoz Laboratory in 1938, LSD was originally developed for medical use as a circulatory stimulant. Because its psychological effects mirrored psychosis, it was used as a research tool on mental illness.

There's one infamous Wu show where everybody in the group was way, way fucked up. It was New Year's Eve, at the Culture Club in Brooklyn, New York. We tore the club up that night—gunshots, everything. There was a lot of Staten Island niggas up in Brooklyn. And I was the ringleader that night, tearing the whole place up that night. No charges were filed. It was ghetto. It was street—whoever got hurt, it was just some street shit. The old days was better, there wasn't no suing or nothing. If you fucked a nigga up, a nigga got fucked up. If he fucked you up, you got fucked up. That was it.

$C_{11}H_{15}NO_2$
3,4-methylenedioxy-N-methamphetamine (MDMA)

AKA: ecstasy, X, XTC, E, M

Patented in 1912 by a German drug company, MDMA was first considered an appetite suppressant, although its usefulness proved limited due to its profound psychological side effects. These include euphoria, a heightened awareness of one's self and surroundings, drastically increased levels of empathy and communication, and a desire to hug up on people and things.

I've tried E, ecstasy. Some hip-hoppers have rebelled against it, saying it make thug niggas soft, but I don't know. I will say it makes you feel real nice, just kissing all over your girl. And I've also noticed E is good for performance. I know I can get onstage and I can rock all night and just *love* the crowd. Take an E pill, you might just rock that show.

I know. I had to leave that shit alone 'cause that shit was killing me. So I had to find a way to get in that trance state of mind again without the narcotics.

My beats travel like a vortex
Through your spine to the top of your cerebrum cortex
Make you feel like you bust a nut from raw sex
Enter through your right ventricle, clog up your bloodstream

— RZA, "TRIUMPH," *WU-TANG FOREVER*

C_2H_5OH
Ethanol (Alcohol)

AKA: Henny, Courvoisier, 40s, O.E., St. Ide's, Shaolin, Wu-Tang

---

Produced by humans for over twelve thousand years, alcohol has been a part of society since before recorded history, used in rituals and customs, banned as a vice or mass produced as a commodity.

Way back in 1990, Ghostface had found the Wu-Tang kung-fu film on his own and he'd be drinking 40 ounces and calling it "Wu." In my hood they called Olde English "Wu-Tang." So I said I didn't drink Wu-Tang, I drink "Shaolin." So Ballantine Ale became Shaolin. This went on for months.

C_4H_{10} (Butane)
$C_6H_5CH_3$ (Toluene)
C_6H_{14} (Hexane)
"Volatile Substances"

AKA: bag, glade, gluey, huff, kick, medusa, toncho, whip-pets, whiteout

---

Volatile substances are products that contain chemicals which, if inhaled, cause intoxication. These products typically contain either the chemical butane or the chemical toluene, although a number of other chemicals are also effective. Intoxication can include euphoria, disorientation, unconsciousness, giddiness, hallucinations, loss of motor skills, slurred speech, heart palpitations, seizures, nausea, and vomiting.

I remember when a cousin took me to a kung-fu flick on Forty-second Street and the kid sitting next to me was sniffing glue. I didn't know what he was doin' at the time, but I could smell it. Later on at school they showed this educational cartoon called *No, No, Pinnochio*, where they showed a guy sniffing glue—and the voice-over guy said "No! No! Pinnochio!"

No, No, Pinnochio!—That was dope. But that was when I realized that the motherfucker next to me had been sniffing glue.

H_2O
Water

One of the essential components of life and the most common substance on earth. After forty-eight hours without water, a human life ends. On the average, a person takes in about sixteen thousand gallons of water during their life.

You know, with a lot of Wu-Tang music, you don't have to listen too hard to know some kind of substances were involved in its creation.

People have called my shit trippy, or stoney, or psychedelic or whatever. But there's some of my work that's very precise, very straight.

"Gravel Pit" is an example. That's a whole different vibe. In a way, it's a sober beat. Everything is precise, it's succinct. One, two—one, two. You know? It's a clean beat.

$C_6H_{12}O_6$
Fructose

Used as common sweetener since the early 1970s, when a Finnish sugar company developed a method to efficiently synthesize it from cane and beet sugar. Now six American companies make fructose from corn. High-fructose corn syrup is made by treating dextrose with enzymes.

You have to see all this in context. The media and politicians will talk about drugs all day, but they don't talk about the other substances that are out there affecting people just as much. You got to look at it as a chemistry project.

A kid in the projects will go to the corner store and spend a quarter and get a pack of Now & Laters, Lemonheads, or some other block of sugar and poison. He'll add a pack of sunflower seeds with a whole bunch of salt, some fried corn chips, wash it down with a Sun Dew drink—which is full of mad artificial flavors, colors, fructose. Then you go get a bunch of chicken wings. What is that? You can't expect good to come out of him when you putting shit like that in. That's bad chemistry.

What I say you got to do, whoever you are, is you need to balance that equation.

All substances are poisons; there is none which is not a poison. The right dose differentiates a poison and a remedy.

—PARACELSUS (1493-1541)

One of his central philosophies was that one should achieve pleasure and avoid pain through clarity of balance of mind and thought. His moral philosophy was a qualified hedonism, advising people to cautiously balance the claims of each pleasure against the evils it may cause. His science considered all of nature as bodies and space—some bodies being atoms, some being compounds of the atoms. Epicurus wrote a study of the natural sciences. It was said to fill thirty-six scrolls.

Raekwon is the Wu-Tang's resident slang master.

WU-SLANG LEXICON

TERMS

Abbot the superior of a monastery, originally from the Aramaic "Abba," meaning "Father"

Ac Acura, typically with reference to the Acura Legend

amarredos small, Italian-styled cookies served with meals

anthidium manicalcum a subspecies of killer bee

apis mellifera a subspecies of killer bee

Apocrypha the famed "lost" books of the Bible, such as Enoch, Maccabees, etc.

applehead a big penis

backwood a type of cigar used for rolling blunts

bag up 1) to be arrested by the police. 2) to have sexual intercourse with

bamma (also bammer) 1) a gun (as in nickel-plated bamma) 2) a country person

beamer a BMW driving machine; "325i's" connotes the 3-series with 25 liter engines; "735i's," "740i's," "750i's" connote the 7-series; the 750iL is the flagship, and "850i's" connotes the BMW 850i coupe

the beast police

bellevue crazy

belly of the beast jail, the justice system

bent high

Bethlehem Brooklyn

biscuit gun

biter appropriator of another man's style (also see shark nigga)

black chocolate African-American female

blue Tahoe a truck

Bojangles a club in New York

bolos South American throwing weapon

boo girlfriend

Book of Enoch a book of the Bible's Apocrypha that tells of the coming Messiah, fallen angels, prophecies, and more

boom marijuana

Box in Hand a kung-fu training exercise in which the student attempts to snatch a box from his master's hand

brolic style rough, fly, big

Brooklyn House a jail in Brooklyn

Brooklyn Zoo Brooklyn

buckshot shotgun shell

burner gun

butter pecan an attractive woman of Puerto Rican descent

cakes kilos

calico gun

clingers prison inmates

c-cipher-punks police

cipher 1) circle 2) surroundings, neighborhood

cheddar money

chef cocaine cook

cherry head idiot

chickenhead a woman eager to dispense oral sex

chips money

chrome gun

Clarks manufacturer of the Wallabee

cockblock to prevent someone from having sex

Coqui 900 a malt liquor

crab a scavenger

crane style 1) a kung-fu style in which the arms are kept wide and make winglike movements, high kicking, and the cranes beak 2) a hand weapon made by joining the fingertips tightly together

cream money, as in Cash Rules Everything Around Me (C.R.E.A.M.)

crill crack

C.R.I.M.E. Criminals Robbin' Innocent Muthafuckas Everytime

Crooked-I sipper one who drinks the nonalcoholic St Ide's beverage Crooked-I

Cuban linx niggas who link together, because Cuban links are strong links

cuffies cousins (comes from an actual name, Cuffy)

darts rhymes/styles

The Desert Queens, NY

Desert E The Desert Eagle, a model of gun

dick rider 1) someone that tries to suck up 2) one who blindly follows artists without any objectivity

dipped well dressed; refers more to clothing than jewelry

dripped wearing a lot of gold and jewelry

drizzy, drizzie a reference to cooking up crack and the cook-up looks weak in the jar like a light snowfall, like drizzle

drop science, drop knowledge demonstrate wisdom or skill

duck sucker

duck seazon hunting for ducks (see duck)

dulses bullets

dumb, deaf, and blind people who have not yet learned or adhered to the ways of the Nation of Gods and Earths

dun 1) used like the word "son" ("What up, dun?") 2) very dark, used in a negative setting, as in dark and ugly

Dutchmaster a brand of cigars often used for rolling blunts

fish pussy

Flavor Wallabees Wallabees that have been dyed a dope variety of colors

flow off to keep mobile, moving away from a given spot

four-nine police

GCC General Civilization Class in the Nation of Gods and Earths

game street-savvy *savoir faire*

gates places where drugs are sold, such as crack houses and weedspots

generator moneymaker

Gilligan fisherman hat

glacier of ice big diamonds

God degree food

God hour seven o' clock

God U's guns

gold fronts vampire-style gold teeth

Gotham New York City

government cheese welfare

gravedigga one who is trying to awaken the mentally dead

grill mouth

gully ghetto style

haggler 1) one who bothers someone else; 2) a bald-headed person, who looks like boxing champ "Marvelous" Marvin Hagler

Hasmonian member of Maccabean family or dynasty

hater one who dislikes someone for no reason other than jealousy

heaterz guns

herb 1) an individual that is easily dissed, robbed, or otherwise violated 2) marijuana

herbalz marijuana

high numbers many years

hollows hollow-point bullets, which explode on impact

ice 1) drugs, particularly cocaine 2) diamonds
ice cream 1) *see* "ice" 2) an attractive woman
ice grill to give someone a mean look
immobilarity 1) I Master More Opponents By Implementing Loyalty And Respect In To Youngsters 2) real property, tangible assets, i.e., real estate

jakes police
jewels knowledge
Jim Kelly black kung-fu actor from the '70s
Jungle Nilz Mariners Harbor (Staten Island neighborhood)

K.B. Killa Beez
Kevlar a bullet-resistant material used for armor on vests and helmets
keys kilos, typically of cocaine
Khadija the Prophet Mohammed's wife
Killah Hill Park Hill housing projects
killer bees *anthidium manicalcum:* this is the most aggressive territorial bee known; male often kills any bee who enters his territory; this bee represents the core members of the Wu-tang clan; *megachile willughbiella:* comes from Kenya, an enormous family with thousands of species commonly called Mason Bees; they represent other artists and groups under the Wu-tang family

knuckle up to get ready to fight, by closing one's fist and opening it or popping one's knuckles

laced paid
Lebanon Long Beach
licking off shooting a gun
liquid swords verbal weaponry
Lo Goose short for Polo goose down jacket; back in the day, Polo gooses were the flyest you could have, costing three to four hundred dollars
lucci money
Luger German gun used by the Nazis in World War II

MGT Muslim Girl Training, teaches how to be a righteous woman
MPV Multi Purpose Vehicle, favored by groups because of their large seating and cargo capacity
Maccabees 1) Jewish dynasty that ruled Palestine aproximately 141 B.C. to 37 B.C. 2) two books of the Old Testament Apocrypha that tell of the Maccabees revolt over Syria
MACS Mac-10 or 11 gun
madhatter drug dealer
Magellan a rapper inventing new styles, after the explorer
Manchus Manchurians, the invaders of China and oppressors of Shaolin in ancient legends
Mecca Harlem/Uptown
Medina Brooklyn
megachile willughbiella subspecies of the killer bee

metal lungies true-to-life lyrics

milk the cow to bestow knowledge upon the youth

money anyone whose name you don't know

mug head or face

New Jerusalem New Jersey

Now Born New Brighton (Staten Island neighborhood)

Old Earth mother

only built 4 Cuban linx only made for those who understand

oowop an Uzi semiautomatic machine gun

oxes razor blades

peace Positive Enlightenment Always Corrects Errors; Proper Equality Activates Controlled Emotions; Positive Energy Actives Constant Elevations; Protons Electrons Always Cause Explosions; Positive Energy Always Corrects Errors; Protons, Electrons, Atoms Cause Explosions

pelican 1) gun 2) bullet

Pelon the Bronx

pie pussy

PJ's housing projects

PLO Palestine Liberation Organization

politic/pollyin' running affairs by verbally making connections and wielding influence

power-U pussy

rainbow dough money from around the world

Red Hook 1) a record label that drops bootleg albums 2) an area in Brooklyn

relish marijuana

ruckus a disturbance or commotion

Ruler Zig-Zag-Zig Allah RZA

scrape to have sex

scuds bullets, after the Scud missiles used in the Gulf War

seed child

shadowbox 1) to spar with an imaginary opponent 2) a form of Shaolin kung fu

shark nigga one who copies another man's style

sheik a leader of an Arab or Muslim tribe, village, or family

shimmy ass

shines gold chains

S-I-N-Y Staten Island, New York

slug bullet, or more specifically the actual projectile part of a bullet

Sing-Sing a New York prison

snakes devilish, untrustworthy, or otherwise shady people

Son of Man a term used to describe Jesus in Revelations

soul controller the controller of all things around one

stunner a show-off

stymied high

sun, moon, and stars man, woman, and child

Sunshower Judgment Day

swayze to disappear, like a ghost, after Patrick Swayze

t'ai chi the martial art that you use to meditate and to expand your mind

Tek 9 a powerful handgun

Thai stick a kind of marijuana

tical marijuana, from the Native American tribe "Tikal"

Timberlands footwear of choice for the winter months

toast gun

trees marijuana

trout pussy

UFOs anyone not from your neighborhood

Vegas cigars, from Garcia Vega

vicked robbed

Vigor car

wagon a standard SUV

walk the dog to take care of business, as in walking one's dogs, or feet, i.e., pounding the pavement

Wally's Wallabees

weight amount of product

whale a heavy shipment

whammy reference to the TV game show *Press Your Luck*

what the blood clot an expression of confusion of Jamaican origin, referencing menstrual cycles, but commonly adapted to mean "what the hell?"

whip car

wig a synechdochical reference to the head

wildflower pussy

Wild Wild West West Brighton (Staten Island neighorhood)

Winter Warz The Cold War

Wu-Tang Witty Unpredictable Talent And Natural Game; We Usually Take All Niggas' Garments; We Usually Take Another Niggas' Garments; Wisdom of the Universe and the Truth of Allah for the Nation of the Gods; Wisdom Unlocks Taught Ambitions, Nurturing Gods

Yard a three-year sentence

NUMBERS

1 and 2 turntables

10 an automatic weapon (see Mac 10)

10% the enlightened yet still wicked

1200 1) the Technics SL 1200 turntable 2) the SP-1200 sampler

1555 the year the first slave ships arrived in America

186, 187 penal code numbers for homicide

2-4 a prison sentence of two to four years

20 1) a $20 bag of marijuana 2) 20-inch rims

211 police code for armed robbery

212 New York area code

226 police code for drugs

24 24-inch rim, usually for SUV or truck wheels

25 with an L a prison sentence of 25 years to life

30 a .30-caliber handgun

357 a .357 magnum handgun

38 1) a .38-caliber handgun 2) "38 hot": angry

4-pound a .45-caliber gun

4-9-3-11 a numerical-alphabetical representation of the word "dick"

40 1) a 40-ounce bottle of malt liquor 2) a .40-caliber handgun

411 information, from the U.S. phone number for information

4:20 the time to smoke marijuana

4:21 another time to smoke marijuana

4:22 yet another time to smoke marijuana

5-0 1 police

5 on it 1) a $5 bag of weed 2) a hand, or five fingers, as in "I got my hand on it"

5% the percentage of enlightened, righteous people on the planet

5-plated nickel-plated

64 1) a 64-ounce bottle of malt liquor 2) a 1964 Chevrolet Impala

8-ball 1) Old English 800 malt liquor 2) an eighth of an ounce of cocaine 3) aware of goings on—i.e., "on the 8-ball" 4) the last ball to be sunk in a pool game, and as such a representative of luck

808 1) the bass sound of a Roland TR-808 drum machine 2) the penal code for disturbing the peace

85% the deaf, dumb, and blind majority of the planet

86 to kill a plan or action, to expel a patron

9 nine-millimeter handgun

900 Coqui 900 malt liquor

950 The Akai S-950 sampler

971 HOT 97, A CHR-turned-hip-hop station in New York

BOOK

THREE

SONG
"PROTECT YA
NECK"

ALBUM
ENTER THE
WU-TANG
(36 CHAMBERS)

[INTRO]

"So whassup man?"

   "Coolin man"

"Chillin chillin? Yo you know I had to call, you know why

   right?"

   "Why?"

"Because, yo, I never ever call and ask, you to play somethin'

   right?"

   "Yeah"

"You know what I wanna hear right?"

   "Whatchu wanna hear?"

"I wanna hear that Wu-Tang joint."

   "Wu-Tang again?"

"Ahh yeah, again and again!"

This was a listener call-in on a City College radio station at 137th Street. Another moment later on the album, where Meth breaks down the members of the clan, was also from radio, an underground hip-hop show on WNYU, out of New York University. We recorded every appearance back then, because there was always freestyling, philosophizing, and clowning.

★SOUNDS OF FIGHTING★

"Wu-Tang Clan comin' at ya . . ."

　　"Watch ya, step kid . . . Watch ya step, kid"

"Protect ya neck, kid . . ."

　　"Watch ya, step kid . . . Watch ya step, kid"

"So set it off."

　　"Watch ya, step kid . . . Watch ya step, kid"

"De Inspector Deck"

[Inspectah Deck]

I smoke on the mic like smokin' Joe Frazier

The hell raiser, raisin' hell with the flavor

Terrorize the jam like troops in Pakistan

Swingin' through your town like your neighborhood Spiderman

So uhh, tic toc and keep tickin'

While I get ya flippin' off the shit I'm kickin'

The Lone Ranger, code red, danger!

Deep in the dark with the art to rip the charts apart

The vandal, too hot to handle

Ya battle, you're sayin' "Goodbye" like Tevin Campbell

Roughneck, Inspector Deck's on the set

The rebel, I make more noise than heavy metal

An ill boxer—the heavyweight champ from '70 to '73 and the first one to beat Muhammad Ali. Every MC feels like a boxer, because the mentality is the same: You know you're the best.

Tevin Campbell was the thirteen-year-old R&B singer who had the hit "Goodbye" back in '91.

[RAEKWON]

The way I make the crowd go wild, sit back, relax, won't smile

Rae got it goin' on pal, call me the rap assassinator

Rhymes rugged and built like Schwarzenegger

And I'ma get mad deep like a threat, blow up your project

Then take all your assets

'Cause I came to shake the frame in half

With the thoughts that bomb shit like math!

So if ya wanna try to flip go flip on the next man

'Cause I grab the clip and hit ya with sixteen shots and more I got

Goin' to war with the meltin' pot

[METHOD MAN]

It's the Method Man for short Mr. Meth

Movin on your left, aah!

And set it off, get it off, let it off like a gat

I wanna break full, cock me back

Small change, they puttin shame in the game

I take aim and blow that nigga out the frame

And like *Fame* my style'll live forever

Niggaz crossin over, but they don't know no better

But I do, true, can I get a "suuue"

Enough respect due to the one-six-ooh

I mean 0, yo check out the flow

like the Hudson or PCP when I'm dustin'

There's a double meaning: He's going to foil your plan, or literally, he's going to blow up your whole housing project, Timothy McVeigh-style.

His thoughts can be as explosive as the wisdom in the Divine Mathematics.

Either sixteen bullets or sixteen bars or lyrics—a deadly verse

New York City, so-called melting pot of different cultures.

He sings that line like a military drill in bootcamp because he's taking MCs to basic training

Reference to the 1980 movie about the New York City Performing Arts High School. In the theme song they sing, "I'm gonna live forever!"

The Shaolin call: "Suuuuuuuue." We used to holler that outside a building to get a nigga to come out, or in a club when there's a fight, to get your people at your back.

That's the building 160 in the Park Hill projects. It was the center—where we did business, hung out, and some of us lived. It was the heart of everything.

The Hudson River and the effects of PCP on an MC's brain—both have mad flow.

Niggaz off because I'm hot like sauce

The smoke from the lyrical blunt makes me *cough*

[U-God]

Ooh, what, grab my nut get screwed

Oww, here comes my Shaolin style

True—B-A-ba-B-Y-U

to my crew with the "suuuuue"

[Ol' Dirty Bastard]

Yeah, yeah, yeah . . .

Come on, baby baby

Come on, baby baby

Come on, baby baby

Come on . . .

[RZA]

Yo, ya best protect ya neck

[Ol' Dirty Bastard]

First things first man you're fuckin with the worst

I'll be stickin' pins in your head like a fuckin' nurse

I'll attack any nigga who's slack in his mack

Come fully packed with a fat rugged stack

Shame on you when you stepped through to

U-God's nickname, Baby U, or Baby Huey

He'll attack any nigga whose game isn't tight, anyone who's slipping, sleeping, or falling off.

A stack of bills or lyrics.

The Ol' Dirty Bastard straight from the Brooklyn Zoo

And I'll be damned if I let any man

Come to my center, you enter the winter

Straight up and down that shit packed jam

You can't slam, don't let me get fool on him man

The Ol' Dirty Bastard is dirty and stinkin'

Ason Unique rollin' with the night of the creeps

Niggaz be rollin' with a stash ain't sayin'

Bite my style I'll bite your motherfuckin ass!

[GHOSTFACE KILLAH]

For cryin' out loud my style is wild so book me

Not long is how long that this rhyme took me

Ejectin' styles from my lethal weapon

My pen that rocks from here to Oregon

Here's more again, catch it like a psycho flashback

I love gats, if rap was a gun, you wouldn't bust back

I come with shit that's all types of shapes and sounds

And where I lounge is my stompin' grounds

I give a order to my peeps across the water

To go and snatch up props all around the border

And get far like a shootin' star

'Cause who I are, is dim in the light of Pablo Escobar

Point blank as I kick the square biz

There it is you're fuckin with pros and there it goes

Both the center of his neighborhood and the center of his rhyme cipher. If you step into the ring in battle, you'll get frozen out by people not feeling you. But also, if you enter his hood, you enter a winter war—get made into a cold stiff.

An early ODB alias.

Ghost was a fast writer back then. He actually wrote this rhyme the night of the recording. Now he takes his time more.

That's really true with Ghost's lyrics: They are colorful and abstract, their sound and shape as important as their meaning

Every nigga in the street game knew about Pablo Escobar, the world's richest, most powerful drug lord, head of the cocaine trade in Colombia until he got killed in '93. He was a real Scarface and Rae and Ghost were deep into those stories.

He keeps his business dealings straightforward.

We can assume Jesus had mad flow because he could rock any crowd. Like the Sermon on the Mount, he had hundreds of niggas captivated—just him, alone, on a mountaintop.

One hundred men, in biblical language.

I never said I follow all of Christ's teachings to the letter.

The black unemployment rate is more than twice that of whites. And it's kept growing and growing since the '60s.

Cold Chillin' records signed GZA in '89 and put out his solo joint, *Words from the Genius*. The label had Kool G Rap, Marley Marl, Big Daddy Kane—lots of giants—but they didn't always know what to do with artists. GZA had a frustrating experience with them, just like I did with Tommy Boy. We both realized we were better off together.

A twenty-watt light bulb only produces a very dim 210 lumens (the measurement of light). These rap labels didn't have enough light force, enough wisdom.

[RZA]

Yo chill with the feedback black we don't need that

It's ten o'clock ho, where the fuck's your seed at

Feelin' mad hostile, ran the apostle

Flowin' like Christ when I speaks the gospel

Stroll with the holy roll then attack the globe with the buckus style

The ruckus, ten times ten men committin' mad sin

Turn the other cheek and I'll break your fuckin' chin

Slayin' boom-bangs like African drums, we'll be

Comin' around the mountain when I come

Crazy flamboyant for the rap enjoyment

My clan increase like black unemployment

Yeah, another one dare, G-Gka-Genius

Take us the fuck outta here

[GZA]

The Wu is too slammin' for these Cold Killin' labels

Some ain't had hits since I seen Aunt Mabel

Be doin' artists in like Cain did Abel

Now they money's gettin' stuck to the gum under the table

That's what ya get when ya misuse what I invent

Your empire falls and ya lose every cent

For tryin to blow up a scrub

Now that thought was just as bright as a 20-watt light bulb

Should of pumped it when I rocked it

THE
WU-TANG
MANUAL

Niggaz so stingy they got short arms and deep pockets

This goes on in some companies

With majors they're scared to death to pump these

First of all, who's your A&R

A mountain climber who plays an electric guitar?

But he don't know the meaning of dope

When he's lookin' for a suit and tie rap

that's cleaner than a bar of soap

And I'm the dirtiest thing in sight

Matter of fact bring out the girls and let's have a mud fight

Artist and Repertoire, the cat who's supposed to be your representative at the label.

That's some definitive whiteboy shit. It identifies someone with no understanding of street ghetto culture.

Literally and figuratively: He doesn't know his slang—doesn't know the meaning of the word "dope"—but also can't tell when something is dope.

★SOUNDS OF FIGHTING★

[OUTRO]

You best protect ya neck

You best protect ya neck

You best protect ya neck

You best protect ya neck

SONG
"BRING DA RUCKUS"

ALBUM
ENTER THE WU-TANG (36 CHAMBERS)

This dialogue is from the kung-fu flick *Shaolin vs. Wu-Tang*, part of the foundation.

I shouted this verse at the top of my lungs at a recording session at Firehouse Studio at 28th Street in Manhattan, with the whole crew in the house. I had a few meanings in mind. I was thinking about having everybody in the whole club or in the neighborhood just go crazy. But at the same time, I was calling out all challengers.

Ghostface just set it off lovely here, so I went with him first. As a result, this is one of the most famous darts in Wu-Tang history, from the first swordsman you meet on the album.

[INTRO]

"Shaolin shadowboxing, and the Wu-Tang sword style

If what you say is true, the Shaolin and the Wu-Tang

could be dangerous"

   "Do you think your Wu-Tang sword can defeat me?"

"En garde, I'll let you try my Wu-Tang style"

[RZA]

Bring da motherfuckin' ruckus—

Bring da motherfuckin' ruckus—

Bring da mother—bring da motherfuckin' ruckus

Bring da motherfuckin' ruckus

[GHOSTFACE KILLAH]

Ghostface, catch the blast of a hype verse

My glock bursts, leave in a hearse, I did worse

I come rough, tough like an elephant tusk

Ya head rush, fly like Egyptian musk

Aw shit, Wu-Tang Clan spark the wicks an'

However, I master the trick just like Nixon

Causin' terror, quick damage ya whole era

Hard rocks is locked the fuck up, or found shot

P.L.O. style, hazardous, 'cause I wreck this dangerous

I blow sparks like Waco, Texas

[RAEKWON]

I watch my back like I'm locked down, hardcore

Hittin' sound, watch me act bugged, and tear it down

Illiterate type asshole,

Songs goin' gold

No doubt,

And you watch a corny nigga fold

Yeah, they fake and all that

Carryin' gats but yo, my Clan

Rollin like forty Macs

Now ya act convinced, I guess it makes sense

Wu-Tang, yo suuue, represent

I wait for one to act up

Now I got him backed up

Gun to his neck now, react what?

And that's one in the chamber

Ignite the fuse of a bomb or spark up a joint. With us, the two went hand in hand.

President Nixon was so corrupt that he stole the innocence of a generation—he damaged the whole era. That's a supreme threat: not just to pop you, your crew, and your family—but damage your whole era. Which is what Wu-Tang did.

The Palestine Liberation Organization. We weren't supporting terrorism, we just felt their guerrilla style: machine guns, ski masks, bandanas.

The Bureau of Alcohol Tobacco and Firearms stormed the Branch Davidians' compound in Waco, Texas, in 1993 and burned it to the ground.

This line gets misheard a lot. He's talking about poorly read motherfuckers in the hood.

A double-meaning: 40 Mac-10 guns and 40 Mack trucks.

He's talking about a gun, but "chamber" always has a double meaning for us.

Wu-Tang banger, thirty-six styles of danger

[RZA]

Bring da motherfuckin' ruckus—

Bring da motherfuckin' ruckus—

Bring da mother—bring da motherfuckin' ruckus

Bring da motherfuckin' ruckus

[INSPECTAH DECK]

When we hit the kung-fu flicks up in Times Square, every theater that wasn't playing kung-fu was playing porno. Both of them were hardcore, but with different definitions.

Guns.

I rip it hardcore, like porno-flick bitches

I roll with groups of ghetto bastards with biscuits

Check it, my method on the microphone's bangin'

Wu-Tang slang'll leave your headpiece hangin'

Bust this, I'm kickin' like Seagal, *Out for Justice*

Out for Justice is a martial arts action movie from 1991 that has Steven Seagal as a Brooklyn cop out to avenge his partner's murder by any means necessary.

The roughness, yes, the rudeness, ruckus

Redrum, I verbally assault with the tongue

Murder One, my style shocks ya knot like a stun-gun

I'm hectic, I wreck it with the quickness

Set it on the microphone, and competition get blown

By this nasty ass nigga with my nigga, the RZA

In *The Shining*, "redrum" was "murder" written backward, but it didn't make sense until the scene where you saw it in a mirror. That's how a lot of Wu-Tang lyrics work too— they only hit you in retrospect, after a few seconds.

Charged like a bull and got pull like a trigga

So bad, stabbin' up the pad with the vocab, crab

I scream on ya ass like your dad, bring it on . . .

[RZA]

Bring da motherfuckin' ruckus—

Bring da motherfuckin' ruckus—

Bring da mother—bring da motherfuckin' ruckus

Bring da motherfuckin' ruckus

[GZA]

Yo, I'm more rugged than slaveman boots

New recruits, I'm fuckin' up MC troops

I break loose, and trample shit like a runaway slave while I stomp!

A mudhole in that ass, cause I'm straight out the swamp

Creepin up on site, now it's *Fright Night*

My Wu-Tang slang is mad fuckin' dangerous

And more deadly than the stroke of an axe

Choppin through ya back [*swish*]

Givin' bystanders heart-attacks

Niggas try to flip, tell me who is him

I blow up his fuckin prism

Make it a vicious act of terrorism

You wanna bring it, so fuck it

Come on and bring the ruckus

And I provoke niggaz to kick buckets

I'm wettin' CREAM, I ain't wettin' fame

Who sellin' gain, I'm givin' out a deadly game

It's not the Russian it's the Wu-Tang crushin'

Roulette, slip up and get fucked like Suzette

Bring da fuckin' ruckus . . .

The boots that the slaves wore in the fields. They're dirty, rugged, and very fucked-up.

A horror movie from '85 about a pair of modern-day vampires moving in next door.

A prism is a pyramid-shaped piece of transparent glass that refracts and separates beams of light. That's also how a mind focuses thoughts and impressions, so GZA means he's destroying a competitor's mind, but also that he's freeing it.

For a long time, everyone assumed that he's just using the term "Suzette" generically, just to mean any old ho. But I actually do remember a girl named Suzette from Shaolin. And I do think she got fucked a lot.

[RZA]

Bring da motherfuckin' ruckus—

Bring da motherfuckin' ruckus—

Bring da mother—bring da motherfuckin' ruckus

Bring da motherfuckin' ruckus

[Outro: Wu-Tang Clan]

So bring it on . . .

So bring it on . . .

So bring it on . . .

So bring it on . . .

So bring it on . . .

So bring it on . . .

So bring it on . . .

punk nigga!

SONG
"C.R.E.A.M."

ALBUM
ENTER THE
WU-TANG
(36 CHAMBERS)

[INTRO: RAEKWON, METHOD MAN]

"What that nigga want God? . . . Word up, look out for the

cops . . ."

"Cash rules"

"Word up, two for fives over here baby . . . Word up, two for

fives—niggaz got garbage down the way . . . Word up.

KnowhatI'msayin?"

"Cash Rules Everything Around Me . . . CREAM get—"

"Yeah, check this ol' fly shit out . . . Word up."

"Cash Rules Everything Around Me"

"Take you on a natural joint"

"CREAM get the money"

"Here we, here we go"

"Dolla-dolla bill y'all"

"Check this shit, yo!"

He means the side of black life you always see reported in the newspapers—crime, death, murder. The side Rae and all of us grew up on.

I grew up on the crime side, the *New York Times* side

Staying alive was no jive

This has nothing to do with a clock. It means hand-me-downs, secondhand clothes.

Had second hands, moms bounced on old man

So then we moved to Shaolin land

His mother left his father.

A young youth, yo rockin' the gold tooth, 'Lo goose

Polo Ralph Lauren down jackets—fly niggas had to have those.

Only way I begin to G off was drug loot

The only decent living came from selling drugs.

And let's start it like this son, rollin' with this one

And that one, pullin' out gats for fun

A blunt mixed with cocaine.

But it was just a dream for the teen, who was a fiend

Started smokin woolas at sixteen

Rushing a known drug-selling spot and either jacking niggas for their loot or taking over the corner yourself. That's high stakes: You might make a lot of money or you might get killed.

And running up in gates, and doing hits for high stakes

Making my way on fire escapes

No question I would speed, for cracks and weed

The combination made my eyes bleed

No question I would flow off, and try to get the dough all

Back in the day, a lot of niggas from Park Hill went to New Dorp High School, where there was always racial tension.

Sticking up white boys in ball courts

My life got no better, same damn 'Lo sweater

Times is rough and tough like leather

Figured out I went the wrong route

He's moving up in the world: getting with a well-connected drug ring and moving kilos of coke from international sellers.

So I got with a sick ass clique and went all out

Catchin' keys from across seas

The Mazda MPV was the hottest minivan back then.

Rollin in MPV's, every week we made forty G's

Yo nigga respect mine, or anger the Tek-Nine

Ch-chick-POW! Move from the gate now

[METHOD MAN]

Cash Rules Everything Around Me

CREAM

Get the money

Dollar dollar bill y'all

Cash Rules Everything Around Me

CREAM

Get the money

Dollar dollar bill y'all

[INSPECTAH DECK]

It's been twenty-two long hard years of still strugglin'

Survival got me buggin', but I'm alive on arrival

I peep at the shape of the streets

And stay awake to the ways of the world 'cause shit is deep

A man with a dream with plans to make CREAM

Which failed; I went to jail at the age of fifteen

A young buck sellin' drugs and such who never had much

Trying to get a clutch at what I could not . . . could not . . .

The court played me short, now I face incarceration

Pacin'—going upstate's my destination

Handcuffed in back of a bus, forty of us

Life as a shorty shouldn't be so rough

But as the world turns I learned life is hell

In one verse Deck takes you through the whole cycle of street life: from scrambling on the street, to hustling, to trying to teach the youth a better way and them not hearing you—and showing how there's no answer.

Deck was twenty-two when he wrote the rhyme. Rae gets a lot of credit for the realness of this joint, but Deck's impressions here are some of the most vivid and real you'll ever hear.

Most long-term prisons in the New York area are upstate.

Living in the world no different from a cell

Police. ▌ Every day I escape from |jakes| givin' chase, sellin' base

Smokin' bones in the staircase

Though I don't know why I chose to smoke sess

I guess that's the time when I'm not depressed

But I'm still depressed, and I ask what's it worth?

He asks his mother about life. ▌ Ready to give up |so I seek the Old Earth|

Who explained working hard may help you maintain

to learn to overcome the heartaches and pain

We got stickup kids, corrupt cops, and crack rocks

In a drug-controlled area, the ▌ and stray shots, |all on the block that stays hot|
whole block is hot—everyone is a
potential target.

Leave it up to me while I be living proof

To kick the truth to the young black youth

But shorty's running wild smokin' sess drinkin' beer

And ain't trying to hear what I'm kickin' in his ear

Neglected, but now, but yo, it gots to be accepted

That what? That life is hectic

[OUTRO: INSPECTAH DECK]

Niggas gots to do what they gotta do, to get a bill

YaknowhatI'msayin?

'Cause we can't just get by no more

Word up, we gotta get over, straight up and down

Cash Rules Everything Around Me

CREAM

Get the money

Dolla dolla bill y'aauhhhaaaauhhhhahhhauhhhhll, YEAH

SONG
"TRIUMPH"

ALBUM
WU-TANG FOREVER

Osiris was the chief god of ancient Egypt, the all-seeing eye and the ruler of the underworld. So ODB is declaring himself the ruler of the hip-hop underworld.

In the Divine Mathematics, the combination of nine and seven signifies God-Born. It's a serious number, a turning point in history.

We would say this to all the girls when we were kids back in 1979, calling off the balcony

Socrates taught that when you're searching for knowledge, you begin by defining all known terms. Deck's saying his disses defy the comprehension of even the most complete set of philosophical knowledge.

Shoguns are the warriors that ran Japan from the twelfth to nineteenth centuries. They were soldiers enforcing the Emperors' reign, but they were also rulers themselves. That's like the nine generals of the Wu-Tang Clan.

[OL' DIRTY BASTARD]

What y'all thought y'all wasn't gon' see me?

I'm the Osiris of this shit

Wu-Tang is here forever, motherfuckers

This ninety-seven?

Aight my niggaz and my niggarettes

Let's do it like this

I'ma rub your ass in the moonshine

Let's take it back to seventy-nine

[INSPECTAH DECK]

I bomb atomically, Socrates' philosophies

and hypotheses can't define how I be droppin these mockeries,

Lyrically perform armed robbery

Flee with the lottery, possibly they spotted me

Battle-scarred shogun, explosion when my pen hits tremendous,

Ultra-violet shine blind forensics

I inspect you, through the future see millenium

Killa Bees sold fifty gold sixty platinum

Shacklin' the masses with drastic rap tactics

Graphic displays melt the steel like blacksmiths

Black Wu jackets queen Bees ease the guns in

Rumble with patrolmen, tear gas laced the function

Heads by the score take flight, incite a war

Chicks hit the floor, die-hard fans demand more

Behold the bold soldier, control the globe slowly

Proceeds to blow swingin' swords like Shinobi

Stomp grounds and pound footprints in solid rock

Wu got it locked, performin' live on your hottest block

[METHOD MAN]

As the world turns, I spread like germs

Bless the globe with the pestilence, the hard-headed never learn

It's my testament to those burned

Play my position in the game of life, standin' firm

On foreign land, jump the gun out the fryin pan

Into the fire, transform into the Ghostrider,

A six-pack and A Streetcar Named Desire,

Who got my back?

In the line of fire holdin back, what?

My peoples if you with me where the fuck you at?

Forensic detectives use ultraviolet light to detect gunpowder, explosive resins, and other traces of a crime scene. But he's the Inspector, so he can blind the forensics themselves. Note that Deck is spinning all this long before the advent of CSI.

That means that female Wu-Tang affiliates—who don't get patted down as much at the door—sneak guns into the club.

A videogame that has a ninja who could pull out a sword, slice someone up, and put the sword away—all in one move.

He's saying he's like a chesspiece—holding down his square. But he's also talking about knowing your role, filling it fully, with faith and reason.

One of his Meth's names, taken from the alter-ego of the Marvel Comics character Johnny Blaze—so it's an alter-alter ego.

This kind of line is typical of Meth in that it's multilayered. It could mean that he's drunk in a theater watching *A Streetcar Named Desire*. Or it could mean he has a six pack of beer in his car, named Desire.

Trying to mess with his head.

Niggaz is strapped, and they tryin' to twist my beer cap

It's court adjourned, for the bad seed from bad sperm

Herb got my wig fried like a bad perm,

What the bloodclot, we smoke pot, and blow spots

Another Meth nickname, for his ability to consume massive amounts of weed smoke.

You wanna think twice, I think not

The Iron Lung ain't got ta tell you where it's coming from

A World War II movie about a huge Nazi artillery unit the British had to destroy.

Guns of Navarone, tearing up your battle zone

Rip through your slums

[CAPPADONNA]

I twist darts from the heart, tried and true

Loop my voice on the LP, martini on the slang rocks

Certified chatterbox, vocabulary 'Donna talkin'

Tell your story walkin'

He's got the drop on you—he's got his gun out first, ready to squeeze the trigger.

Take cover kid, what? Run for your brother, kid

Run for your team, and your six camp rhyme groupies

He's saying, "Your martial arts are basic compared to mine." You have to watch the sentence endings with Capadonna; they fall in funny places.

So I can squeeze with the advantage, and get wasted

My deadly notes reign supreme

Your fort is basic compared to mine

His verses are packed with time-release poison that takes effect after consumption. They affect you in a delayed reaction after you've heard them.

Domino effect, arts and crafts

Paragraphs contain cyanide

Take a free ride on my dart, I got the fashion

Capadonna is even more deep into fashion than Raekwon. His closet itself is a catalog.

catalogs for all y'all to all praise to the Gods

"The saga continues

Wu-Tang, Wu-Tang"

[U-GOD]

Olympic torch flaming, we burn so sweet

The thrill of victory, the agony, defeat

We crush slow, flamin' deluxe slow

For, Judgment Day cometh, conquer, it's war

Allow us to escape, hell glow spinning bomb

Pocket full of shells out the sky, Golden Arms

Tunes split the shitty Mortal Kombat sound

The fateful step make, the blood stain the ground

A jungle junkie, vigilante tantrum

A death kiss, catwalk, squeeze another anthem

Hold it for ransom, tranquilized with anaesthesias

My orchestra, graceful, music ballerinas

My music Sicily, rich California smell

An axekiller adventure, paint a picture well

I sing a song from Sing-Sing, sippin on ginseng

Righteous wax chaperone, rotating ring king

[RZA]

Watch for the wooden soldiers, C-Cypher-Punks couldn't hold us

A thousand men rushin in,

A U-God nickname.

Other rappers' beats sound like cheap sound-effects from a Mortal Kombat videogame.

U-God's temper is infamous inside and outside Wu-Tang Clan.

He's using this to mean exotic and flavorful.

The aroma of pungent California-grown greenbud.

The first part is saying this record (wax) is a righteous guide (chaperone) through life.

"Ring King" has a triple meaning: a CD or record, a kung-fu fighting style, and an old school boxing video game called Ring King.

In the Laurel and Hardy movie *March of the Wooden Soldiers*, there was an unstoppable army of wooden soldiers—they just kept coming and coming. I'm saying the Wu-Tang is that army.

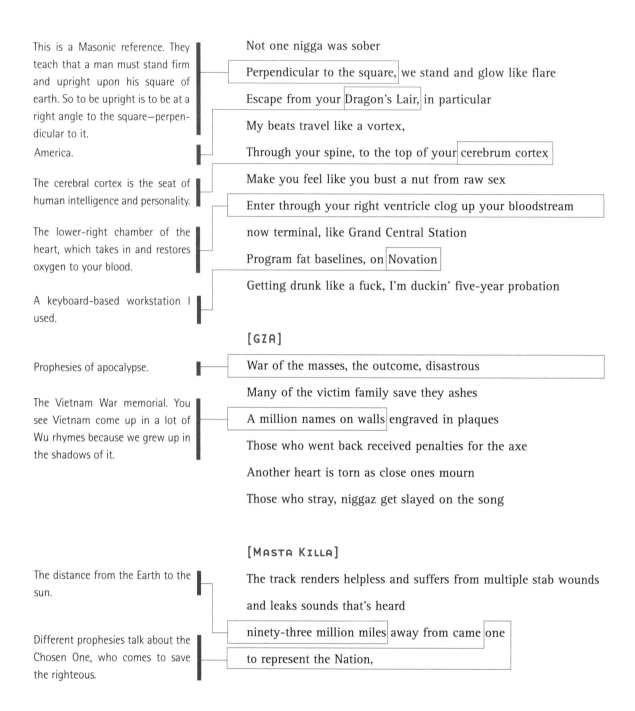

This is a Masonic reference. They teach that a man must stand firm and upright upon his square of earth. So to be upright is to be at a right angle to the square—perpendicular to it.

America.

The cerebral cortex is the seat of human intelligence and personality.

The lower-right chamber of the heart, which takes in and restores oxygen to your blood.

A keyboard-based workstation I used.

Not one nigga was sober
Perpendicular to the square, we stand and glow like flare
Escape from your Dragon's Lair, in particular
My beats travel like a vortex,
Through your spine, to the top of your cerebrum cortex
Make you feel like you bust a nut from raw sex
Enter through your right ventricle clog up your bloodstream
now terminal, like Grand Central Station
Program fat baselines, on Novation
Getting drunk like a fuck, I'm duckin' five-year probation

[GZA]

Prophesies of apocalypse.

The Vietnam War memorial. You see Vietnam come up in a lot of Wu rhymes because we grew up in the shadows of it.

War of the masses, the outcome, disastrous
Many of the victim family save they ashes
A million names on walls engraved in plaques
Those who went back received penalties for the axe
Another heart is torn as close ones mourn
Those who stray, niggaz get slayed on the song

[MASTA KILLA]

The distance from the Earth to the sun.

Different prophesies talk about the Chosen One, who comes to save the righteous.

The track renders helpless and suffers from multiple stab wounds
and leaks sounds that's heard
ninety-three million miles away from came one
to represent the Nation,

This is a gathering of the masses that come to pay respects to the

Wu-Tang Clan

As we engage in battle, the crowd now screams in rage

The high chief Jamel-I-Reef take the stage

Light is provided through sparks of energy

from the mind that travels in rhyme form

Givin' sight to the blind

The dumb are mostly intrigued by the drum

Death only one can save self from

This relentless attack of the track spares none

[GHOSTFACE KILLAH]

Yo! Yo! Yo, fuck that, look at all these crab niggaz laid back

Lampin' like them gray and black Pumas on my man's rack

Codeine was forced in your drink

You had a Navy Green salamander fiend

Bitches never heard you scream

You two-faces, scum of the slum

I got your whole body numb

Blowin' like Shalamar in eighty-one

Sound convincin', thousand dollar cord by convention

Hands, like Sonny Liston, get fly permission

Hold the fuck up, I'll unfasten your wig, bad luck

I humiliate, separate the English from the Dutch

Masta Killa's righteous name.

The ignorant are first attracted to Wu-Tang wisdom by hearing the beat. That's the first step.

Those were *the* classic early-80s Pumas. He's saying suckers are profiling like they're as fly as those old kicks.

A wack type of footwear.

An R&B group formed by the booking agent from Soul Train. They were blowing up until '81, when the lead singers quit.

A $1,000 microphone cord—the epitome of a pimped-out MC.

Another ill boxer, heavyweight champ from 1962-64

The Dutch and English were the main founders of New York, but this also refers to Dutchmaster cigars and Old English malt liquor.

LYRICS

159

Genovese is a chain of New York drug stores, always well-stocked and often selling items in three-packs.

Two-layered: A Caesar salad needs vegetables to exist; an emperor needs money to rule.

Again, the distance from the Earth to the Sun, but in this context it means that the woman, the earth, is distant from the Man, who is the first.

Megahertz measure the cycles per second of any electronic device, but now it usually refers to the power of a computer's central processing unit. So he's saying he destroys your computer, blows your mindframe.

To notarize means to make things official. That's what Rae does as an MC: Locks it down and keeps it real.

A style of jewelry Rae rocks: a tarantula made out of white gold. That's some old playa shit.

He's saying the beat is heavy and strong like a diesel truck.

The point guard of the Toronto Raptors, originally of the New York Knicks; known for beautiful assists.

It's me, black nobled you Ali

Came in threes we like the Genovese, is that so?

Caesar needs the greens

It's Earth

Ninety-three million miles from the first

Rough turbulence, the wave burst, split the megahertz

[Raekwon]

Aiyyo that's amazing, gun in your mouth talk, verbal foul hawk

Connect thoughts to make my man-child walk

Swift notarizer, Wu-Tang, all up in the high-riser

New York Yank' visor, world tranquilizer

Just a dosage, delegate my Clan with explosives

While, my pen blow lines ferocious

Mediterranean, see y'all, the number one draft pick

Tear down the beat God, then delegate the God to see God

The swift chancellor, flex the white-gold tarantula

Track truck diesel, play the weed God, substantiala

Max mostly, undivided, then slide in, sickenin'

Guaranteed, made 'em jump like Rod Strickland

ALBUM
WU-TANG
FOREVER

* This was a song title listed on
GZA's *Liquid Swords* for a song
that didn't actually manifest until
Wu Tang Forever.

[INTRO]

"The Wu-Tang Clan will rise again.

There are many of us, working for the good of the Wu-Tang."

"Die!"

★SOUNDS OF FIGHTING★

Refers to a classic kung-fu flick from
the '70s, starring the Yuen brothers
and showing a lot of tight choreography with fighting poles, or staffs.
One warrior used a fishing pole as
his staff, another used a deadly staff
known as the Hell's Wind.

[STREET LIFE]

So get your egg crashed, by my Hellz Wind Staff

While the feature broadcast is splashed to tell the news

like Katie Chung, how the bullet collapsed his lung

She was a local New York newscaster.

His father watched the horror as he swallowed his tongue

Another youth dead, before the age of twenty-one

Left his son to grow, in the ghettos of the slums

With a shot that go, for twisted metal for cash flow

React slow nigga and get P.L.O.

In this usage that just means get
clipped—assassinated.

By the lone gunner, who took revenge for his brother

who got slain last summer by a cocaine runner

A new year is dawning, new crews is forming

He's breaking down the cycle of revenge, showing how it might never end.

Rival gangs warring, blood steadily pouring

The streets are deep, Son, every day is like a rerun

So I reach out and try to teach one

This means that society's content is 85 percent mentally deaf, dumb, and blind people. But it also means that these people are content, that ignorance is bliss.

But eighty-five percent uncivilized content

No tolerance so a lifetime is spent

behind a cage bent smoked out on a park bench

Killer instinct slave rap niggaz get lynched

SOUNDS OF FIGHTING

[GHOSTFACE KILLAH]

So yo break that nigga arm fast as a fuck

Tell Raekwon Goldie left my beige jacket in his truck

Small feet with a big body—awkward and clumsy.

To all you slew footed penguins, duckin' from these

Self-described evil MCs, from the name of the devil's son in the 70's horror-flick *The Omen*.

hot rocks that's flamin, chocolate for all you rap Damiens

That's what Rae planned to name his next solo joint, but a lot of people misheard this lyric as "Seth Abraham."

Spraying cards espionage, dodgeball square hard

Strip bars, no bras, wet leotards

and a mink in, next album "Blood on Chef's Apron"

In the most famous story in the Book of Daniel in the Old Testament of the Bible, Daniel is sent to the lion's den because he was caught praying. But Daniel just walked out without any of the lions touching him.

Keep a Gambino PlayStation in your playpen

Discovery Channel, cats the Book of Daniel

Coke blunts hot as a fuck swatted bamboo

high school dropouts, baseheads get knocked the fuck out

on the regular for robbin' a good nigga house

Rough cut raw doses, the unexplainable

Hot rock lava, gringo throw the Frusen Gladjé

SOUNDS OF FIGHTING

[Inspectah Deck]

Ha ha ha ha, yo

What you know about this, specialist armed dangerous

Hit you close range with this madness

Unique design shine like a deep dish

The beat kick technique split all your weak shit

Yes, the rhythm, the Rebel

Alone in my level heat it up past the boiling point of metal

Living legend, veteran known to set trend

Lethal weapon, step through your section

With the Force like Luke Skywalker

Rhyme author, orchestrate mind torture

Live performer, bid the mic "Sayonara"

Borderline to insane, I rain firewater

Tape recorder, can't be saved by a court order

I got my sword cross your throat you joke

[Method Man]

We on the run with the golden guns, get you none

When it reach out and teach someone, blaze they buns

A brand of ice cream you saw everywhere back in the '80s. It was shady—they tried to make it sound all Scandinavian after Häagen Dazs blew up, but it turned out to be American.

He's quoting the first line of the Public Enemy joint, "Rebel Without a Pause."

A reference to the '70s James Bond flick, *The Man with the Golden Gun*, which had Christopher Lee playing the world's most expensive assassin.

Now I'm guilty by association

Times of blackness eclipsin' the sun, target practice

Commence when I throw these darts at these rappers

Ricochet, hit the charts, bloody your mattress

Hold me down, Wu bloodkin, I'm goin' in

Shootin' bullets at the top ten, rhyme concoction

blend like a million

All these niggaz want cheese, is we mice or men, word up

We can go platinum but then, still can't get no satisfaction

Once again, back on the block crumb-snatchin'

Blowin backs in cold

Blunted non-assassin, time for action, Johnny Unitas

Handle that like arthritis

Still, hold a golden touch like King Midas

★SWORDS CLASH★

[RZA]

Drown in problems the Heineken's imported from Holland

Gettin' boosted off a killer bee pollen,

Stone columns get cracked by drum tracks loud as gun claps

Pin a crab nigga to death with a thousand thmb tacks

The Wu centerfold, it bees the *Wind Ninja Scroll*

Soul Edge Blade controls your Interpol

The Fig Newt, fruit from the forbidden tree root

Another double meaning: 1) a mattress as used in *The Godfather*, as a shield. 2) Sexual wreckage in bed.

The family bonds of the Wu-Tang Family.

Money.

He was the legendary quarterback for the Baltimore Colts whose nickname was the Golden Arm. The phrase also plays on the call for Johnny Unite-Us—meaning Johnny Blaze to bring the Clan together.

Bobby Digital's blunts were dipped in his special "bee pollen," which could also mean blunts dipped in ginseng or PCP.

The drum beat is loud enough to shatter stone columns, like Samson shattered stone columns in the Old Testament.

A famous anime film, originally titled *Wind Ninja Chronicles*.

Refers to Soul Blade, a videogame about a supernatural sword in the 16th century that all these warriors are trying to get. Soul Edge was a character you could only play once you had mastered the game.

I stay secluded in the chamber trainin' new recruits

with Fatal Guillotine, the black hooded team what it means

> The hand-thrown spinning sword you saw in old kung-fu flicks. It was the origin of the Wu-Tang logo.

when bullets scream from the hot Glock like rock from a sling

Pushed through like George Bush Operation Wolf

> When either of the George Bushes wanted to go to war they just did it.

Shots get popped on the block cause them blood to gush

> An old video arcade game in which all you did was shoot as many people as possible with a machine gun

From digital to analog, the Wu-Wear camouflage

The entourage squad we stompin through Zanzibar

like herds of cattle, RZA plays the wall like a shadow

> A New York nightclub, but also the commercial center of East Africa and the last place to abolish the slave trade.

Connectin' Brooklyn/Shaol like the Verazanno-Narrows

> The bridge that joins Brooklyn to Staten Island.

[RAEKWON]

Stash the cream though, Isotoner ice style gleamin'

Lex graffiti name Remo, hold 'em we rollin'

> Rae's graffiti tag was "Remo."

> Rae chose this also because Lex, Luther, Superman's arch enemy was super-rich.

askin' me though, raps is hotter than hot tamales in Toledo

Pussy that shit she passin' off to me though

We wax Ajax niggaz with a ax, Maxamill

> Scrub niggas, worthless niggas.

> Maxamillion: a GZA alter-ego.

You could crash a meal, got you back Steel

> Bobbie Steels: a RZA alterego.

Scold em and fold 'em like the thousand dollar bills

Sit back eyein' y'all niggaz out

Fakes that delegate we spittin' fire out

Verb burglar, design the Wally shoe store reserve

a jet status, Guyanese birds up on my mattress

> Girls from Guyana.

Watch me mack this, Ralph Lauren goose inside a fashion

> The mattress is filled with Ralph Lauren down feathers.

Yo, these hands is flooded and they mad quick

Strong approach like magnets, custom wood name

> Covered in diamond rings.

He's flipping the old slapstick bit of a guy slipping on a banana peel on the sidewalk—he's slipping on a Klondike bar instead

Windbreakers were played out.

A quick dis on rap-magazine cowards

Stylin' rich, RZA made the waves in one chain

Feelin' mics like, wheelin' a bike, slide like

step on his Klondike, get your dart right

We movin' on it like, windbreaker niggaz get they face broke

Jewelry get snatched, magazine right on the low, fuck y'all cats

[OUTRO]

★SOUNDS OF FIGHTING★

"May you rot in hell!"

"Ahahahahah, ahahahahaha, ahahahahaha!"

SONG
"IMPOSSIBLE"

ALBUM
WU-TANG FOREVER

[INTRO: RZA AND TEKITHA]

"Yo . . . check check it"

   "You can never defeat"

"Yo check the method of this shit right here one time"

   "The Gods"

"Sparkin' your braincells to the upmost"

   "Impossible"

"Unlimited epidemics bein' spreaded"

   "You can never defeat"

"You know, we try and add on for y'all niggas"

   "The Gods"

"Yo, yo"

[RZA]

Fusion of the five elements, to search for the higher intelligence

Women walk around celibate, livin' irrelevant

The most benevolent king, communicatin' through your dreams

That's a Taoist principle of martial arts, where you strive to bring together the five elements—metal, water, wood, fire, and earth—inside your body to regenerate yourself. But I'm also referring to the book *Fusion of the Five Elements* by Mantak Chia.

Back when I wrote this rhyme, I kept meeting people who said they'd met me in their dreams. So I felt like I was trying to be a benevolent king, visiting people that way.

That atmosphere that surrounds the earth has four distinct layers: the troposphere, which starts at the Earth's surface and extends five to nine miles up—it's where weather happens; the stratosphere, where the ozone layer is; the mesosphere; and the thermosphere, which goes up to 400 miles high and is known as the upper atmosphere. After that, it just blends into outer space.

Society considers a housing project like Stapleton to be a concentration camp—a place you put the unwanted.

A lot of this comes from the *Matrix* series by Valdemar Valerian, five volumes of books that compile reports on how human consciousness is being modified by different institutions, by chemicals added to the food, water, and environment, and by electromagnetic warfare.

Back when Reagan came in, some people theorized he was Satan because his three names—Ronald Wilson Reagan—had six letters each: 6-6-6.

Generic street name for a rich person.

A famous Marvel comic superhero whose duty was to seek out and kill demons disguised as humans.

Mental pictures been painted, Allah's heard and seen

everywhere, throughout your surroundin' atmosphere

Troposphere, thermosphere, stratosphere

Can you imagine from one single idea, everything appeared here

Understanding makes my truth crystal clear

Innocent black immigrants locked in housing tenements

Eighty-five percent tenants depend on welfare recipients

Stapleton's been stamped as a concentration camp

At night I walk through, third eye is bright as a street lamp

Electric microbes, robotic probes

Taking telescope pictures of globe, babies getting pierced with
    microchips

stuffed inside their earlobes, then examined

Blood contaminated, vaccinated, lives fabricated

Exaggerated authorization, Food and Drug Administration

Testin' poison in prison population

My occupation to stop the inauguration of Satan

Some claim that it was Reagan, so I come to slay men

like Bartholemew, 'cause every particle is physical article

was diabolical to the last visible molecule

A space knight like Rom, consume planets like Unicron

Blasting photon bombs from the arm like Galvatron

[U-GOD]

United Nations, gun-fire style patient

Formulatin' rap plural a capella occupation

Conquer land like Napoleon, military bomb fest

We want sanitary food, planetary conquest

Thug peoples on some hardcore body shit

Get your shit together 'fore the fuck Illuminati hit

Dreams is free in escape of sleep

For a fool peep jewels, keep tools for tough time

The rule of rough mind, elevate, stay behind

The sun gotta shine, keep on, cremate

the whole Babylon, times up, move on

Kings on your pawn, checkmate, no fakes

opposed through the gate, case closed

Things get froze, when it comes time, chosen ones

were holding guns, we take flight with no fright

and attack, never fear cause our words is clear

What's been done can't be undone, Son, we can't care

'Cause the last days and times are surely here

Snakes and flakes get flung, by the righteous ones

Divine minds combine and unify as one

Half of black hope, we half broke, smoke a bowl of weed shit

Our everlastin essence' stay flyin' over Egypt

[TEKITHA]

For you to defeat, the Gods

Impossible, you can never . . . defeat

His raps are taking over, conquering and occupying territory, which is the job of every MC.

The moment when the conspiring forces of evil take over the ruling parties of the world. It was prophesized to happen in 2000. You may not believe in prophesy but look at what did happen after 2000.

Wisdom

He's telling niggas to leave the roughness and wildness behind them, to evolve.

Babylon is loaded with meaning. The name means Gate of God. It was one of the biggest ancient cities, located close to where Baghdad is now in Iraq. They had both the Tower of Babel and the Hanging Gardens of Babylon, one of the Seven Wonders of the world. But in the Bible, Babylon represents Paganism, and so it often means any morally corrupt city.

The area around Egypt is the cradle of civilization, which is where the original black Asiatic man first emerged. He's saying that the essence of black man still floats above the region.

The Gods, impossible

For you to defeat, the Gods

*This whole verse is a Ghost classic—for its tight rhymes, emotionalism, and storytelling. It won *The Source* magazine's Rap of the Year award.

[GHOSTFACE KILLAH]

Call an ambulance, Jamie been shot, word to Kimmie

Don't go, Son, nigga you my motherfuckin' heart

Stay still, Son, don't move, just think about Keeba

She'll be three in January, your young God needs you

The ambulance is taking too long

Cellphone.

Everybody get the fuck back, excuse me bitch, gimme your jack

The 9-1-1 emergency number in Shaolin's 718 area code.

One-seven-one-eight-nine-one-one, low battery, damn

Blood comin' out his mouth, he bleedin' badly

Nahhh Jamie, don't start that shit

Keep your head up, if you escape hell we gettin' fucked up

The special day at Yankee Stadium when fans are given free small bats

When we was eight, we went to Bat Day to see the Yanks

In sixty-nine, his father and mines, they robbed banks

He pointed to the charm on his neck

With his last bit of energy left, told me rock it with respect

There was an actual police officer named Lough running wild in Shaolin. He was a regular harasser of us back then—he locked U-God up, chased Meth, and actually killed one of our people. When you hear "Can It Be So Simple," and they say, "Case was killed by the cops," Lough is the cop they're talking about. He was just a mean white kid on some Robocop shit.

I opened it, seen the God holdin' his kids

Photogenic, tears just burst out my wig

Plus he dropped one, oh shit, here come his Old Earth

With no shoes on, screamin' holdin' her breasts with a gown on

She fell and then lightly touched his jaw, kissed him

Rubbed his hair, turned around the ambulance was there

Plus the blue coats, Officer Lough, took it as a joke

Weeks ago he strip-searched the God and gave him back his coke

Bitches yellin, Beenie Man swung on Helen

In the back of a cop car, Dirty Tasha are tellin'   A local ho with a big mouth.

But suddenly a chill came through, it was weird

Felt like my man was cast out my heaven now we share

Laid on the stretcher, blood on his Wally's like ketchup

Deep like the full assassination with a sketch of it

It can't be, from Yoo-hoo to Lee's   That means we grew up together—
                                                       from the chocolate kid's drink Yoo-
                                                       hoo to the junior-high jean Lee's.
Second grade humped the teachers, about to leave

Finally, this closed chapter comes to an end

He was announced, pronounced dead, y'all, at twelve ten

[Outro: Raekwon and Tekitha]

"Now what my man is trying to tell y'all

Is that across the whole globe (you can never)

The murder rates is increasin', and we decreasin' (you can never)

So at the same time, when you play with guns

When you play with guns Son (you can never defeat)

That causes the conflict of you goin against your own (the Gods)

You hear me, so let's pay attention

Straight up and down, 'cause this is only a story

From the real"

SONG
"PROTECT YA NECK
(THE JUMP OFF)"

ALBUM
THE W

[INSPECTAH DECK]

"Ladies and gentlemen, we'd like to welcome to you

All the way from the slums of Shaolin

Special uninvited guests

Came in through the back door

Ladies and gentlemen, it's them!"

Dance with the mantis, note the slim chances

The tennis star was nicknamed "The King of Swing"

Chant this anthem, swing like Pete Sampras

Takin' it straight to Big Man On Campus

Brandish your weapon or get dropped to the canvas

Scandalous, made the metro panic

Cause static, with or without the automatic

ODB was in jail when we recorded this, so we wanted to send him a cut of the proceeds.

And while I'm at it, yo, you got cash, pass it

It's drastic, gotta send half to Dirty Bastard

[Raekwon]

Ayo, ayo

Waves is spinnin', blades is spinnin'

Slay' em in the eighth inning

Stay truck, god stay playin' linen

Kill rap, observe the Uptowns, ho, feel that

Mink jeans on, seen where the real at

2000 zitos, movin' wit a ill ego

For real, for real, ill lines, ill people

Yo, bring it back, nine more civilians

Pollyin' deals, monopoly and bills

Y'all niggas lyin'

Caught 300, lab look royal wit a mean stomach

Go broke, all seen, done it

Words from the heavyset

If I don't eat, then we already met

Fly ass bro, liver than coke

Hair waves—Rae always had good hair.

Lyrical swords are spinning.

Meaning stay heavy, keep your jewelry on. Rae rocked gold cables in that video.

Dressed in fine linen suits.

The fly Nike Uptown kicks.

That's some surrealistic pimp shit.

Mercedes Benz 2000s.

The Wu Tang Clan.

He made 300 grand quickly, his crib is hooked up like a king's, and he's well-fed.

That's Raekwon, he's a heavy brother.

[Method Man]

Now what Clan you know wit lines this ill?

Bust shots at Big Ben like we got time to kill

Niggas can't gel or I'm just too high to tell

Put on my gasoline boots and walk through hell

Wit nine generals, nine ninjas in your video

Nine milli blow, semi auto wit no serial

This is a classic Meth line. He's talking about shooting at the Big Ben clocktower in London to kill time. Kill time—get it?

If you wear gasoline-coated boots in hell, you're one brave motherfucker.

PCP, but also referring to Bobby Digital, the dark side of RZA.

Man metaphysical, I speak for criminals

Who don't pay they bills on time and fuck wit Digital

Never seen, smoke a bag of evergreen

Meth is describing running a basement craps game, taking cash and guns for bet stakes.

My sword got a jones, more heads for the severing

Johnny in the dungeon, takin' all bets, throw ya ones in

Scared money don't make money, throw ya guns in

Damo is the Indian pilgrim who introduced the foundations of Ch'an Buddhism to China, but it's also a shout-out to Killa's son, Damo.

[MASTA KILLA]

That's word to Damo, San Juan, Puerto Rico

That's Killa's lady.

Blowin' hydro on a beach wit Tamiko

My gun bullet hollow for you to swallow

Blow in the nozzle, hear it whistle

One in the head, this is code red, man for dead

He's flipping Carroll O'Connor, who starred in the TV series of *Heat of the Night*, and was also Archie Bunker in *All in the Family*.

X amount of lead spray from the barrel

Heat clear the street like Connor O'Carroll

Fully equipped, rifles, banana clip shit

To make my niggas from East New York flip

Ralph Lauren Polo sneakers

[RZA'S BOBBY DIGITAL]

Those are the fly yellow Havana Joe shoes I always wear.

Yo, you may catch me in a pair of Polo Skipperys, matching cap

Razor blades in my gums

A down-filled jumpsuit, like a snowsuit that was actually carried by Wu Wear.

(BOBBY!)

You may catch me in yellow Havana Joe's goose jumper

I'm talking like I carry a Star Trek phaser, but mine has only one setting and it's not "stun."

And my phaser off stun

(BOBBY!)

Y'all might just catch me in the park playin' chess, studyin' math

Shining seven and a sun

The platinum-diamond Islam star I wear around my neck.

(BOBBY!)

But you won't catch me without the ratchet, in the joint

Smoked out, dead broke or off point

(BOBBY!)

[GHOSTFACE]

Wallo's comfortable, chocolate frosting

Your socks hangin' out, yours is talkin'

Rock so steadily, son, I'm still crazy

Sport my old Force MD furs in the '80's

Force MDs was a Shaolin rap group and the only fly niggas back in the day who had fur coats.

Nat Turners wit burners, Jackie Joyner-Kersee

Nat Turner was a slave that had a religious vision that told him to break free and lead a revolt. He did but his people weren't armed very well—they just had shovels basically. So Ghost is imagining his crew as modern-day Nat Turners, only with guns.

Taught y'all niggas how to rap, reimburse me

The black female Olympic medalist in track and field.

Rothsdale's, ruby red sales, Bloomingdale's blocks

Rothsdale's: a jeweler.

Ox tails chopped up in Caribbean spots

Diamonds.

I'm nice, maxed out, creepin' wit the ax out

Murder these bikini bitches, switchin' with they backs out

A favorite ingredient of West Indian soup

A style of butt-shaking dance women do down in the islands.

[U-GOD]

Niggas wanna pop shit, I pop clips

Bitch, I'll put my dick on ya lips

Alabama split, hammer slay quick

That David Banner gamma ray shit

Some strong green weed, referring to the kind of radiation that altered the biochemistry of David Banner and made him become the Hulk.

Shells in the mouth, jailhouse snitch

My powder voice, Snow White stiff

Cocaine —

Verbal killas, gorilla grip

That means a tight grip on a gun or
an enemy's throat.

God body shit, puff Marley spliffs

[CAPPADONNA]

A Benz, not Cap's kind of ride.

You might see me in a six, that's not my style

You might see me wit a bitch, that's not my child

I be in the Benzo, keep a low profile

Dead serious, take flicks and don't smile

Tryna get money, y'all cats is wild

I pose for the clothes, make a song like wild

I'm a chip off the board game, got sword game

Live life to the fullest, still want more fame

Darts on layaway, beats on standby

Outfits pressed up, ready for airtime

[GZA]

This is a classic GZA verse in the
way that it extends one metaphor
to fill the whole joint. He's talking
about rap as a track event run by
Jesse Owens. His record-setting
time for the 400-meter relay was
7.0 seconds. So GZA is the Jesse
Owens of this.

Run on the track like Jesse Owens

Broke the record flowin', without any knowin'

That my wordplay run the four hundred meter relay

It's on once I grab the baton from the DJ

A athlete wit his iron cleat in the ground

Wildest nigga who sprint off the gun sound

The best time yet still seven-point-zero

Swift flow made the cameramen clothes blow

SONG
"Uzi (Pinky Ring)"

ALBUM
Iron Flag

[U-GOD]

"Yo . . . yeah

Don't erase none of that good shit in the beginnin'

Yo . . . spill drinks on ya, get stank on ya

Yo . . . yo . . . pinky ring shit, yo

That pinky ring shit yo"

> In the mafia, when you get made you get a ring you wear on your little finger that has the mob insignia on it. Around this time we were all into pinky rings.

It's that pinky ring shit, the legend of masked kid

Shoot out the speakers when my guns get Jurassic

> Meaning big like dinosaurs.

Superbad, who am I? Dolemite classic

> U-God rocked that style of lid back then: the classic Dolemite-style, named after the Rudy Ray Moore '70s pimp flicks.

The vandal's back, hands on Angela Bassett

I handle my plastic, gunplay I mastered

> Glocks are plastic-made.

No coke, dope mixed down with acid on record

Broken down and crafted in seconds

> U-God wrote this rhyme quickly.

Ladies' choice, the golden voice still peppered

Better, respect it, bitch believe

I pull rabbits out the hat, tricks up my sleeves

I air out the showroom, the shit can breathe

Fix your weave, behold my expertise

[WU-TANG CLAN]

Everyone had guns back in the hood. But if you had an Uzi, you were the man. Trust me.

I got my Uzi back—you dudes is wack, face it, the Wu is back

I got my Uzi back—you dudes is wack, face it, the Wu is back

[RAEKWON THE CHEF]

A double meaning: the fruit punch they serve in rec rooms, or getting beat up in a rec room.

Take it back to the peoples, leanin' gettin' rec room punch

Trading cars in an alleyway.

We in them authentic alley switchin' joints

Major general niggaz, five stars

Both arms rock when coke dropped

We read a hundred niggaz palms

Silencers, garbage bags of hash

He's saying we have ex-cops working for us now.

For every cop we paid retired now the nigga on smash

Gash you out your burner fast

You swing down hatin' me now respect

Get your fingers off the glass

[CHORUS]

[GHOSTFACE KILLAH]

Yo what the fuck yo?! Yo what the fuck y'all comin for?

Get the fuck away from my door!

We got big guns in here, coke over there

With blue bag and E pills stashed under the chair

And there's Boss Hog black and white pit with the pink lips

Stan thought he was soft 'til he bit his fingers

The shit had me dyin' yo, big fat nigga bleedin'

Big cat nigga all season

On the beach truck, stuck with Hawaiian Ice

Diamond twice the whole city thought I bought FUBU

Blew you, authentic doodoo, picture the fog iced out

Eighteen karat rap between noodles

[CHORUS]

[RZA]

Up at Killa Bee headquarters, full rips is poured up

I saw Johnny sippin' Henny from a iced out cup

Yo with the blunt, two-way vibratin' off the hip

I sit, took three drags off the honey-dip

Now what you talkin'? You see my gold fronts sparkin'?

Ain't tryin to hear what you dogs be barkin'

Read the headline, that was blast on today's *Post*

Dead King, thought he could ace Ghost

Queen, couldn't even jack Monk

Probably find him in Doc Doom's back trunk

Bdoodoodoo! I'm up at the Wu library

Readin Malcolm's . . . *Any Means Necessary*

A description of a pitbull, but it could also mean a white cop, with a reference to the corrupt Southern mayor Boss Hogg in Dukes of Hazzard.

His rep was so large, people assumed he'd bought the clothing company FUBU.

Noodles can mean a hat but also Masta Killa is known as Noodles, so this line can mean he's dropping verses between Killa's verse and someone else's. I'm known to change the order of the verses around at a late stage, so that could be how he conceived it.

The 36 Chambers recording studio in midtown Manhattan.

An extended metaphor based on playing cards, it's the story of a punk nigga who thought he was a king, but he was really a bitch-ass Queen, and got taken out by Wu-Tang affiliates Black Knights (Monk and Doc Doom).

There is a Wu Library and it currently resides at my crib.

A collection of speeches, interviews, and letters by Malcolm X. It's different from *The Autobiography*, which was actually written by Alex Haley. It was published in 1970, after he died and it's the raw material—straight from Malcolm.

[METHOD MAN]

That's a tight line—he's John John like New York, New York.

John John, Bacardi straight up hold the ice

So nice like New York they had to name him twice

Name your price, I black out then change the lights

Give you the same advice that I gave my wife

Don't fuck with mine, Clan give you lumps in nine

Let the smoke cloud clear so the sun can shine

That's the Wu Tang Clan itself—a nine-nigga culture shock.

Culture shock, for some of us that's all we got

Whether you ball or not, you can all be shot

[INSPECTAH DECK]

New York, New York, legendary rhyme boss

Code name Charley Horse, bust with blind force

I smash set it and wreck for cash credit or check

A welterweight champion from Brooklyn who is real quick. He dances when he fights.

You crabs test, can't measure the threat

I dance on a nigga like my name's Zab Judah

Much bigger than a Big Kahuna—a XXXL Kahuna.

Rap barracuda, three XL kahuna

Sure to get it perkin' and 'cause a disturbance

I'm thirstin', feel what I feel then we can merge then

Move contraband through the country by stashing it in cars with big engines.

Creep it through the states in V8's and 12's

My weight's hell, fuck with me then brace yourself

The Noble, Sir I mass mogul

Known to blast vocals, and move global on you locals

[MASTA KILLA]

This is grown man talkin', coward I split your head

I'm from the East where the streets run red from the bloodshed

Hit Chef for the rice and peas

Nuff respect Father E tumbled at ease

My brothers can't wait to squeeze the automatic

They need wreck like a drug dealer need a addict

Floatin on the 95, sting like a killer bee

Your hands can't hit what your eyes can't see

[GZA]

From dark matter to the big crunch

The vocals came in a bunch without one punch

Rare glimpse from the, strictly advanced, proved unstoppable

Reputation enhanced, since the cause was probable

So you compare contrast but don't blast

through extreme depths, with the pen I hold fast

Watch the block thirst for one became all

Shot 'em with the long forgotten rainfall

Delivered in a vivid fashion with simplicity

The blind couldn't verify the authenticity

The rhyme came from the pressure of heat

Then it was laid out, on the ground to pave streets

[OUTRO]

I got my Uzi back . . .

I got my Uzi back . . .

That's E-Tone, who owns a restaurant in Jamaica, Queens that Masta Killa frequents.

This is flipping Muhammad Ali's most famous dart: "Float like a butefly/Sting like a bee/No one can beat/the greatest Ali." He changed it up to talk about a drug trafficker driving Route I-95, which runs from all way from Maine to Florida.

The Big Bang, the birth of the universe.

A punch-in is a technique used in studios to fix performance mistakes. He's saying he doesn't need them.

That's the Wu-Tang, raining ancient knowledge and wisdom on the needy.

GZA's early rhymes were famous for being simple and intense.

The mentally blind, deaf, and dumb keep sleeping on it.

SONG
"RULES"

ALBUM
IRON FLAG

Some old Wu darts edited to together to make one verse: "Both hands clusty" [Ghost], "Pullin out gats" [Raekwon]/"Double barreled" [Meth], "Blew off the burner kinda dusty" [Ghost]/"We back, don't test" [Raekwon] "Bring it to 'em proper, potnah" [Meth]/"Comin' from the thirty-six chamber" [Meth]/"Math, let the plate spin" [GZA], "Many brothers y'all be sparkin'"/"Stray shots, all on the block that stays hot" [Deck], "If ya fuck with Wu, we gots ta fuck wit you" [Method Man]

The Twin Towers of the World Trade Center, 1973-2001. R.I.P.

[RZA]

All you hos, be cryin' for these bitches

All you niggaz, be cryin' for these hos

★SCRATCHED SAMPLES★

[GHOSTFACE KILLAH]

Who the fuck knocked our buildings down?

Who the man behind the World Trade massacres, step up now

Where the four planes at, huh, is you insane bitch?

Fly that shit over my hood and get blown to bits!

No disrespect, that's where I rest my head

I understand you gotta rest yours true, nigga my people's dead

America, together we stand, divided we fall

Mr. Bush sit down, I'm in charge of the war!

[INSPECTAH DECK]

Yes yes y'all, the I-N-S bless y'all

Stop hearts like cholesterol, let's brawl

Never fall, tear it down like a wreckin' ball

Roll call where my niggaz that's one for all

And all for one, we draw the guns on impulse

Cash in the envelope, spend it on kinfolk

Then smoke a ounce as we count mills

Providin' you pure ecstasy without pills

[METHOD MAN]

Y'all know the rules, we don't fuck with fools man

How the fuck did we get so cool, man?

Never ever disrespect my crew

If ya fuck with Wu we gots to fuck wit' you

[MASTA KILLA]

Y'all dogs better guard ya grills, it's all real

We live from hills it's the God I-Reelz ——————————— ▌ A cat from Brooklyn Killa knows.

Yo Wonderful, spark the billz

——————————————————————— ▌ Light the blunts

Let me build with the people for the mills

I'm rollin with the Rebel I-Ill from Killa Hill, peace to ▌ Park Hill housing projects on Staten
    Brownsville   ▌ Island.

Brothers that'll kill for the will of the righteous

Twenty-five to lifers, true and livin' snipers

You wait like Six Sextil 'til hard to kill

That's worplay on "weight" and "wait." The earth's weight is sextillion tons.

[STREETLIFE]

How you livin' StreetLife? I'm surrounded by criminals

Serial killers tote guns without the serial

High-tech, street intellect, all digital

Project original, sheisty individual

New York's bravest, always supply you with the latest

We hall of famers, and still hit you with the greatest

Took a year hiatus, now you wanna hate us

Thanks to all you haters for all the cream you made us

He's flipping on the phrases New York's Bravest, which refers to New York's firemen, who everyone was talking about after 9/11, and New York's Finest, which refers to the cops.

[METHOD MAN]

Y'all know the rules, we don't fuck with fools man

How the fuck did we get so cool, man?

Never ever disrespect my crew

If ya fuck with Wu we gots to fuck wit' you

[RAEKWON]

Sendin' letters to China, my cousin in Wendy's on Viacom

At home, it's worth money, I adorns

Order drinks, all real niggaz order your minks yo

We got the fitteds on, lookin' all fink

Daddy everybody get money from now on

Payday flash Visas livin' like, Easter e'ryday

Don't fuck Benz, rather a four thirty

That shit that float through water, eyeball come up, drop birdies yo

[METHOD MAN]

We can eat right, or we can clap these toys

I'm with StreetLife, ain't never been a Backstreet Boy

Who y'all kiddin? Tryin to act like my shoe fittin'

Confused with ya head up yo' ass like who's shittin'?

It's Hot Nixon, same team same position

Battin' average three-five-seven and still hittin'

Y'all still bitchin', still lame and still chicken

I'm still here, one leg missin' and still kickin'

Cause I'm haaaaaaaaaaaard! Hard like a criminal

Love like a tennis shoe, throw slug to finish you

It's the Method Man, for short Mr. Meth

I can tell this motherfucker ain't Wu, look at his neck

★SCRATCHED SAMPLES★

"Comin from the thirty-six chamber" [Meth] "Bring it to em

proper, potnah" [Meth] "Wu, Tang, Wu, Tang"

Another Method Man pseudonym, flipping off Hot Nickels

That's a very good batting average, but also a 357 Magnum.

A reference to Das-EFX joint "Hard Like a Criminal"

Brings back a Method Man dart that was in the lead-off mix.

[METHOD MAN]

It's Wu-Tang, rushin yo' gang, crushin' the game

Pretty thugs, clutchin they chain, hand cuppin they thang

Who get strange, gassed up playin' with flames

Let a nigga take off his shades, see what I'm sayin' is . . .

[OUTRO: METHOD MAN]

Y'all know the rules, we don't fuck with fools man

How the fuck did we get so cool, man?

Never ever disrespect my crew

If ya fuck with Wu we gots to fuck wit' you

BOOK

FOUR

WU-TANG SAMPLES

If there's something to steal, I steal it!

—PICASSO

I feel that we have the sound of our generation in the records we made. Al Green, Isaac Hayes, and those niggas—that sound is in the records. It's all there if you want to find it, almost like the Rosetta stone. In one Wu-Tang album you get twelve different kinds of inspiration. You could make a whole album based on "C.R.E.A.M.," and it could be a good album. Years from now you could take any one of those songs and put on an album and realize that the album was inspired by that. I put out hundreds of beats that were completely different from each other, so a producer could easily take one sound from my work and just run with it.

The sampler is a tool and a musical instrument. That's how I always thought about it. Even though I've learned how to play a lot of other instruments over the years, I still feel that the sampler is an instrument that I *play.*

When I first started producing, the only person I knew doing the kind of bugged-out sampling I was into was Prince Paul—him and maybe a few other guys. I still think that first De La Soul album, *3 Feet High and Rising,* is a masterpiece. Paul and I have been friends since 1988. He even programmed the hi-hats on my first single on Tommy Boy.

I never thought about imitating his style, but he did show everybody that you could take anything with a sampler—cartoons, children's records, French lessons—and make it musical. I'm a kung-fu fiend, so I would sample from kung-fu movies, but also, if I'm walking down the street and see a *Peter Pan* vinyl sitting on the ground, a man selling it for a dollar—I'm buying that. If I see a *Flintstones* record for a dollar— I'm buying that. Anything. I buy it, I listen to it, and start hearing the phrases inside of it. And then, I'm sampling it.

In New York City, the Village was the place to find your ill records. That, or you could go to Beat Street Rock 'n' Soul. And on West Forty-third in Times Square, you had the Music Factory. It doesn't exist anymore, but that was the hip-hop spot. That's where you could find every break beat, every dope hook, all types of funk. When I found that store, I just went crazy.

I'm like that even now with records. Once Wu-Tang went on tour, while other guys went chasing girls, I'd just go record shopping. I bought a lot of records out of Switzerland, France, all over the world. I dropped ten grand in Switzerland on one trip, just on records. I got the record I used in "Gravel Pit" in France, when I was living there in a villa in 1998. That's from a French film soundtrack for the movie *Belphégor*—that Antoine Duhamel shit. I stayed there maybe four months and I was producing a lot of beats there, and that was one of them.

I feel like I have all types of signatures to my style, so I don't have one particular sound. I know that a sound I became known for at the beginning was that detuned acoustic piano zither—those solo creepy notes that quiver in the air. It's the kind of sound you hear in "7th Chamber," "Da Mystery of Chessboxin'," and a bunch of other early joints. It's funny when people ask me the inspiration for it, because, to be honest, it was jazz pianists—mostly Bill Evans and Thelonious Monk—but the fact is I played most of it myself.

Early on, I saw that movie *Straight, No Chaser*—a documentary about Thelonious Monk. I watched it and saw how this guy was playing and it was just . . . *crazy*. I mean, he'd play a note or two. Smoke a cigarette. Smack the piano. Walk away from it, come back. And it was like, "You can do anything! There's no rules to it!"

After I saw that movie, I started playing around with the piano part in "Chessboxin' "—where it goes "DO, doo-do-DOO. Doodle-DOO. Do. Doo." You hear me try to go up a little bit, flip it out a bit. That's all from me watching Thelonious Monk with a joint in my hand, just playing.

The piano is detuned because I sampled the note that I was playing. It couldn't be in tune because they didn't have the time-stretching then. Back then, if you sampled a note and played it on another key of the keyboard, you couldn't keep the same BPMs. Now you can. But back then, I just thought it sounded dope that way. That's the other lesson: The limitations of technology can become artistic tools themselves. They can point the way.

A lot of people still don't recognize the sampler as a musical instrument. I can see why. A lot of rap hits over the years used the sampler more like a Xerox machine. If you take four whole bars that are identifiable, you're just biting that shit. But I've always been into using the sampler more like a painter's palette than a Xerox. Then again, I might use it as a Xerox if I find rare beats that nobody had in their crates yet. If I find a certain sample that's just incredible—like the one on "Liquid Swords"—I have to zap that! That was from an old Willie Mitchell song that I was pretty sure most people didn't have. So certain songs I just jacked.

But on every album I tried to make sure that I only have 20 to 25 percent sampling. Everything else is going to be me putting together a synthesis of sounds. You listen to a song like "Knowledge God" by Raekwon: It took at least five to seven different records chopped up to make one two-bar phrase. That's how I usually work.

As far as dialogue samples from kung-fu flicks or crime movies, I'm also pretty careful. Sometimes, now and then, I'll hear a hip-hop joint throw in a sample of some Al Pacino shit and it sounds completely random. It doesn't have anything to do with the song itself.

I always try to have a dialogue sample be part of the story we're telling. I look for something that says what we're talking about in the music or what the song's about. When it comes to movies, it takes me months, if not years, of holding something in my head, thinking I might use that one day.

The one thing I always go back to is that the first sampler that I used—and that I continue to use daily—is my mind. I go watch movies, or I listen to records, or check out songs—I might not make a beat for a week, but I'm listening to the music all that week. I'm sampling it in my mind.

TECHNOLOGY

Computers are useless. They can only give you answers.

— PABLO PICASSO

To my soundwave there's no sonic solution

No Pro Tools to edit or out-date my producin'

— RZA, "CHI KUNG," *BIRTH OF A PRINCE*

In hip-hop, you must master the technology. If you don't, you're dependent—either you're a slave to the technology itself, or to the niggas you need to run it for you. Whenever you can, you should make sure that you're the one in the driver's seat.

But at the same time, once you learn it, you can forget it. That's the ultimate goal: to not think about it, to just feel your way through the machine. That's where you want to be. But sometimes you find you have to take some shortcuts along the way.

I got the money for my first piece of equipment by selling newspapers on the Verrazano Narrows Bridge, the bridge that links

In 1857, Leon Scott patented an invention called the "phonauto-graph." It used a horn to focus sound waves onto membranes that were attached to a hog's bristle. The device inscribed the sound onto the visual medium, although it had no way to play it back. In 1878, Thomas Edison patented an invention called the "phonograph," which could both record and replay sound, inscribing it on a vertical cylinder. In 1887, Emile Berliner patented his "gramophone," which also recorded and replayed sound, only on a horizontally placed disc. Horizontal discs proved easier to mass produce, and in 1895, Berliner began commercial production of his disc records and "gramophones" or "talking machines" to play them. Although both cylinders and discs were sold from the mid-1890s to the late 1910s, the disc system gradually became more popular due to cheaper price and better marketing.

Brooklyn to Staten Island. When I was around twelve, my partner and I ran this scam on commuters. We'd sell them only the outer comics section and fill the rest of the paper with the coupon part. So after we sold those on the bridge, we'd go bring the rest of the paper back to deli owners, who'd buy them and return them to the printers for credit. I took the money that I got from that and bought my first straight-arm turntable.

After that, I just kept scrambling for more gear. In 1982, I started in the hip-hop world with a straight-arm Technics SL-6 turntable. I got an echo box and a rhythm box. The rhythm box was real basic—just a beatbox where you couldn't even program the drums, you could only press the presets. But it was dope—the same one used in Grandmaster Flash's "Flash Is on the Beatbox." Those were the first three things that I had to make hip-hop.

By 1985, I had a Roland 606. (Actually, a guy we knew had it and we ended up stealing it.) Then after the 606, Roland came with the 707 and I got one of those. (Actually, a famous DJ from Staten Island called Dr. Rock owned one and let me borrow it.) Once I learned how to use the 707—around '85 or '86—I started making demos. The 707 was more like real programming. The 606 was grid programming, but with the 707 you could play it and record it. It had a better interface.

After the 707 came, of course, the 808. A lot of people consider the 808 to be the gold standard of old-school hip-hop—*the* great drum machine. It's true, at the time, everybody was getting those. But I could never afford one. And my DJ, he had a 909. To me, the 909 is a more basic foundation of hip-hop. Everyone loves the 808 for the bass, but the 909 is the one with all the great drum sounds. For example, "I Need a Beat" by LL Cool J. Run/DMC—all that clicking, that BA-doom, DIT, DE-DIT-DIT-DIT-DIT"—that's the 909. That, and another machine, the Oberheim DMX, those beatboxes were essential. These are the first things that I got a hold of.

Finally, I went up to the four-track and the two Technics 1200 turntables. So by '87, I had myself a little studio. It was a Yamaha four-track that I borrowed from my DJ Skane, a Roland 909 drum machine that I borrowed from my other DJ Scotty Rock, and a pair of turntables—1200s. I also had a Casio CZ-101 and a Casio RZ-1—all borrowed, of course.

Once the four-track came out, the power of a home DJ became incredible. Because then I could DJ whichever breakbeat I wanted to use, and then for my next track, I could go back and get another totally different record. So I started to put on bugged-out shit—*Peter Pan* records, *Woody Woodpecker* records, all these weird records that I would use as musical background. And then on the next track I could record my own vocals. With that setup, I'd record about an album a month. Me and ODB, me and Raekwon—we all did albums together at my place. GZA was too good for me to rap with at that time.

THE SAMPLER

By 1988, samplers were being made, but as usual, I couldn't afford one. The only sampler I had would sample for two seconds. It was a Casio toy sampler, the one that they had in the department stores that had four pads on it and could sample for two seconds. It was the first sampling machine Casio ever put out.

I made an album with that machine, though. Since it would only sample two seconds, I would take the turntable and speed it up as fast as possible and then slow the playback all the way down—that was the only way to get a track in. I had a few local neighborhood hits like that.

A sampling drum machine for rap music production, introduced in the mid-'80s. Ced-Gee of the Ultramagnetic MCs is reputed to have been the first person in hip-hop to use this machine, which became one of the most sought after pieces of equipment. Even Young MC has a lyric that goes, "Just me, a mic, and an SP-12." (The SP-12 was a version of the SP-1200 with fewer features.)

One day, a producer named RNS let me borrow a sampler called the EPS, made by Ensoniq. And that changed my whole perspective.

The Ensoniq EPS could sample ten seconds, which was incredible back then. That meant you could get two whole bars—you could do practically anything! RNS let me hold it, without a disc, and I made maybe five or six beats and laid them down on my four-track. That was my first introduction to being a real hip-hop producer.

In 1988, I'd finished recording my single "Ooh, I Love You Rakeem" and a few other songs, and I'd worked with people like Prince Paul, and the GZA had just finished his record *Words from the Genius*. That was when I saw Eazy Mo Bee and his brother using this machine called the Emulator SP-1200.

That machine basically changed my life. Once again, I got it from, you know, malfunctioning—I got it maliciously. I put some money down on it and never continued to pay. I got it without an instruction manual or anything. I stayed up for two days with no sleep and mastered it. Once I mastered that machine, it was *on*. "Bring the Pain" was made on that machine.

I started making a lot of hot beats in the hood. And then that same

Ensoniq EPS

producer, RNS, he wanted to switch up. He let me hold his Ensoniq EPS for a month and I let him hold the SP. And that was another change of the whole game, because I liked the EPS more. The EPS was a keyboard, the SP was a drum machine. The keyboard style became more my style, because I started playing my samples like melodies.

That really wasn't being done by people back then. They would just push the key, drop in the sample, and that's it. They wouldn't usually actually play the sample. But back then, I would start sampling one note and playing it on different notes of the keyboard. I started chopping things down to notes and chords, not knowing which chords they were but knowing them as sounds. That's what *36 Chambers* was mostly made on—the Ensoniq EPS.

After that, they made another one, the EPS-16 Plus. So when that came out, in 1990, I already had a lot of beats—"Bring the Pain" and a whole bunch of other beats—stored inside my SP-1200. Now I had this Ensoniq-16 Plus, which sampled thirty-two seconds, so I could double it up, but now it was sixteen-bit.

If you lower your sample rate—from forty-four to seventeen or twenty—it increases your sample time. So you get to have longer samples, but with lower resolution. That gives more of a grindy sound, because the sound breaks up. If

Ensoniq EPS-16 Plus

you lower the sample rate, that means you're missing some of the frequency of the sample. Years later, I heard people call it "lo-fi," but I just thought it sounded more ghetto and it let me use more sounds. At that time, 70 percent of my music was sample-rated at 17.9.

The SP-1200 was only twelve-bit anyway. So even though it was more advanced, I made the Ensoniq sound *less* advanced. But it gave me more time. It was after the Ensoniq-16 Plus that I basically launched my career.

A year and a half later, in 1991, Ensoniq came out with the ASR-10. Then I was able to sample for maybe sixteen megs, at a sample rate of 20.9, which would give you at least a minute. That was, like, forever! That's when I first made the song "Can It Be So Simple."

The beautiful thing about the ASR-10 is this: It was the first sampler that you could play the beat that you made. I mean, let's say you already made a drum pattern. You could sample while playing your beat. Therefore you could monitor what you were sampling and hear what you were adding on to it. As a DJ, that was perfect. I could scratch in what I wanted and sample and hear it as I did it, and be on beat every time.

When that came into my life, that changed my whole game one more time. You could sample for a minute and change, so I could sample a whole verse. That's what's behind a song like "Shimmy Shimmy Ya," which came out in 1995 but was recorded in 1993. The rap verse

ASR-10

itself is a sample. Dirty rapped into the ASR, so on the second verse he raps backwards—because I just reversed the loop. That unleashed all kinds of imaginative power. I could sample so much stuff into one beat. I'd have a whole complete beat ready to take into the studio.

Another thing that's powerful about the ASR is that it comes with fifty effects parameters, such as rumble filter, guitar amp, Van Der Pol filter—that's why when you hear that bass on "7th Chamber Part II" on *36 Chambers*—that bassline is being played and put through the Van Der Pol and the guitar amp. That's incredible right there.

So with "Can It Be So Simple," you hear the woman's voice at the beginning, saying "Everybody talkin' about the good old days, the good old days . . . let's talk about the good old days . . . " With the ASR, I could have that whole intro and then drop my beat! When Rae and Ghost first came to my house and heard that, they couldn't believe what happened. Basically, that's the foundation of my production career right there.

As time went on, we increased our equipment and got into all types of effects, synths, and processors—Mahley compressors, Behringer compressors, the Nord Lead—it just kept going. Like on the *Liquid Swords* album—all the synth you hear is the Nord Lead, which was made by Clavia. And then Clavia also made this thing called the ddrum. So on *Wu-Tang Forever* you hear a lot of that: drums that aren't sampled but played on the ddrums. So the technology started getting a lot better and I started playing with more toys.

Now, I have thousands and thousands of machines—I have more than thirty keyboards—but I'm not sure if I have a true favorite. I like the Fantom, but I don't have a main keyboard. Still, I have to give a lot of respect to the Kurzweil. The ASR-10 is my favorite keyboard in history, but the Kurzweil would be my second favorite. Also, the Kurzweil can actually read the ASR-10 disc. So when I did *Wu-Tang Forever*, I took all my ASR and EPS discs and just stuck them into the Kurzweil. It's compatible like that, so it's like the overfiend of the whole shit.

I came at music the long way around—from the lo-tech to the hi-tech to, lately, just plain instruments. Over the years, I've studied music, I've studied theory, I've studied composition. Now I'm a pretty cool guitar player, piano player, drummer. On one song in *Wu-Tang Forever*, there's a violin part, and when we were making that, I couldn't even play what I wanted, I just hummed it. The girl that played it, she's the violinist with Yanni—the only person that gets a solo onstage with him.

But later on, I actually composed for orchestra. So it's been a strange evolution. At first, I was interested in more chopping sounds. Then I got more into keyboards. Now, I'm like, "Fuck that. Hip-hop is gonna be able to be played in Carnegie Hall." But not with a DAT—with a hundred-piece orchestra and a turntable. And Bobby Digital is gonna be right there in the middle.

SPIRITUALITY OF PRODUCING

Where the spirit does not work with the hand there is no art.

—LEONARDO DA VINCI

People tell me that they never see me worry. I'm this nigga where there could be a bomb in the room, it's going to go off in fifteen minutes, there's no way we can get out, and I'll just be like, "We're getting out." It's just how I am—I recognize the beauty of Allah. And if you do that, you see an order in everything, the divine in every moment of existence. I've felt that way for years, but it's accessible to all of us. If you grasp it, it's like every breath is sweet.

I think that outlook is a big part of how I produce music. You hear something beautiful in everything around you. You don't think too hard about it—you just take it in, let it out. It's almost like you have to get out of your own way. Dip into the stream, come back out of it with jewels, let them pass through you.

The true work of art is but a shadow of the divine perfection.

— MICHELANGELO

Producing music is a spiritual act. I think anybody that makes music seriously, for long enough, comes to understand that. You know that everything you're doing in life relates to the music you're producing and vice versa.

These days, I'm even aware of which direction I'm facing when I produce—like how Muslims pray to the east. Right now, where I'm working, I'm facing a pond with a waterfall running down in a Japanese garden. The feng shui is popping. It helps you be aware of your surroundings, where you are, what you're going through—to see where you fit into the universe around you.

Inside the hood and the ghetto, there's another kind of spirituality to producing. The aggression and oppression, it can take you out or—if you're in the right mind frame, the right spirit—it can bring something out of your spirit, something wild and raw. If you can let nature into you while you're producing, your music might sound like nature—there's an aggressiveness to it, but there's an ebb and flow, a rise and fall, a pattern. If you're only letting the hood into you, you're going to be stuck with that expression. But either way it's about getting that out of you.

If you listen to earlier Wu-Tang stuff, you hear the aggression and the violence of the hood in the music itself. *Enter the Wu-Tang* basically started with me yelling at the top of my lungs, "BRING THE MOTHERFUCKIN' RUCKUS!" And that's how we felt. Whether we were talking to another crew from another hood, or an officer of the law, or the American government, or some MC who thought he could rhyme, we were just saying "Bring it, motherfucker, Bring it on." That was our spirit at the time.

Those who want to know what sound goes into my music should come to New York and open their ears.

—THELONIOUS MONK

Music is naturally all around us, whether someone's blasting it through speakers, singing it, playing it on a violin—or not. It's always there in the ether. But to me, hip-hop was always different.

From the first time I heard it, I felt it was something that had always been inside me. I remember I was seven years old. And the sounds, the vibe I caught—it felt like it was *in* me already.

It was the summer of '76 and we were in Staten Island. My grandmother lived in 240 and I was visiting her when GZA came over from 55 Boeing. I remember that year, '76, as being the best year of my life.

That night, GZA took me to a block party—had me out till eleven. I shouldn't have been out that late, and I got a whupping. But that night changed my life. It was DJ Jones.

I don't know what else to say. That was it. I saw something that night. I felt some part of me expressed in the air, in the people, and in the world around me.

The way it hit me—it was like an opening of something inside me. Something came from outside and opened up something inside. The DJ was cutting up on two turntables, it could have been the song "Apache"—I remember that being one of my favorite songs at the time—and the rapper, he wasn't saying much. It was just, "I'm twice as nice when I rock the mic," "Yes, yes, y'all," shit like that. A DJ and a rapper, plugged into a streetlamp.

As a kid I remember I'd always read Mother Goose and Dr. Seuss in rhythm. I always did it like that, on my own. And once I heard someone rocking like that, I never stopped. Everything I read from that point on, I read with a mind to rhyming it. I even remember the first rhyme I wrote—it was really just taking something from GZA: "You with the young girl, you like to get fresh/You can hug and squeeze her, slip your hand up her dress." It doesn't sound too heavy now, but it was a beginning.

I started MCing at eight and half, nine years old. I started DJing at eleven. I started producing at sixteen. That's already eight years of graffiti, breakdancing, producing. I lived hip-hop. I rode the trains up and down this city all by myself at seven and eight years old. From Brownsville, Brooklyn right near Betsy Head Pool, we'd ride to Forty-second Street, another slum, and just go wilding. Along that path, we'd come across breakdancers, rappers, graffiti artists, fighters, drug users, drug abusers, drug dealers, squealers, wheelers, dealers, gamblers, dice games, dope fiends, all that.

I went in the South Bronx Soundview Projects with my cousin GZA, listening to people rap. I went all over Staten Island, hanging with the best DJs and rappers at block parties and getting my ass whipped by my mother when I came in. I hung with breakdancers, I wrote graffiti, breakdanced, popped, DJed. All facets of hip-hop that existed, I engulfed myself in. I really lived it. And I express it at any given moment.

On top of that, I've studied a lot. I can't think of anyone else in hip-hop that brings the kind of knowledge I have on such a range of subjects to the game. But it wouldn't matter, if that hip-hop spirit wasn't already inside me. To me, that's the spiritual side of hip-hop.

Art is the elimination of the unnecessary.

—PICASSO

When I was coming up, I never found a producer that could make all the beats I could rhyme to that fit my style. Back then, most producers couldn't MC and most MCs couldn't produce. It's still that way for the most part. To me, it's different. I always hear the music and the rhymes as a whole. That's why I started producing myself.

In the beginning, I had no true understanding of how music works—theory, harmony, chords. I had no idea about the way it's traditionally structured. But in a way, this was one of those rare cases where a *lack* of knowledge was power, because there wasn't anything to get in the way of what I wanted to express. I just took sounds that sounded good to my ear and put them together. They were probably disharmonized and not in sync, but I could feel how they should fit as a whole.

My instinct was to keep it sparse. The sparseness leaves more ideas for the mind. If you notice, when you get a very complex piece of music, your mind tends to follow the music. When you have a sparse piece of music, your mind imagines its own things about the music. It fills in the blanks. It's like a visual artist using negative space.

I feel that I heard something new in the music that nobody was feeling. I heard a temperature, a vibe, a pulse. A lot of it was about being simple and slightly fucked up. If you take my music and separate it track by track, you'll find a lot of it's not on beat. I'm intentionally messing it off the beat—but when it all meshes together it makes another rhythm of its own.

Music only needs a pulse. Even a hum, with a bass and snare—it'll force a pulse, a beat. It makes order out of noise. It'll work with anything, I mean *anything*. To make a song, it doesn't take anything but my will. It's there always in me. Beat. Rhyme. I can always put some-thing together—even out of just one word. I think that's what true pro-ducing is. You find the music in anything. You listen and you can hear it. It's almost like you're just letting the beauty of Allah shine out on its own.

I can't stop producing. It's just something about me—I can't sit still. I have thousands of beats that I can't put out yet. In fact, I don't know if I'll ever put them out. But I just keep making them. It's like breath-ing for me.

Actually producing for me is like many things in nature. It's like what Bruce Lee said about water: "Water can flow or it can crash." It's fluid and moving freely—especially for me, because I have so many different MCs. They help the fluidity of the music. My producing has also had to be like the sun, which has to shine its influence over the planets. All these MCs, I had to please them, appease them, bring the best out of them.

I don't say this just to blow myself up. In a way, I don't look at it as coming from me. I'm more like a channel for it. A channel that has really good reception.

VOICES AS INSTRUMENTS

RZA makes ghetto symphonies. . . . His music has classical elements, but at the same time it's hardcore and street. No one can go from Beethoven to the hood like he can.

—WYCLEF JEAN

I get a Beethoven vibe from him.

—TRIP-HOP ARTIST TRICKY ON WORKING WITH RZA

Number of symphonies composed by Beethoven: **9**

I always thought of the different voices in the Wu-Tang Clan as being instruments. They were the instruments I used to compose. Instead of me having a trumpet player or a bass player, I had Ghostface or U-God. On a song like "7th Chamber," everybody rapping back to back, it's high pitch to middle pitch to bass pitch. Ghost, you could call the soprano, then you take it down to Raekwon and Deck with the tenor, then down to the bass of U-God and ODB. Or it's like Ghostface is the strings: He gets more mellow, more emotional on you, but at the same time, strings can attack.

They're also MCs, though, so every one of the nine generals could play a different composing role at a different time. At one point, Method Man was the hook master: "All my people, are you with me, where you at," or "Cash rules everything around me, get the money, dolla-dolla bill y'all." But at the same time, I'd yell some hooks like "Bring the motherfucking ruckus!" or "Wu-Tang Clan ain't nothin' to fuck with." And then you got Dirty dropping "Shame on a nigga, who try to run game on a nigga." And GZA, when he went "Clan in the front. Let your feet stomp," that shit was *compelling*—something about the way he said it, it made you *do* it. The whole crew is full of talented MCs, so there's no telling what you're going to get out of them.

Over time, though, I got to know which MC would shine on what kind of track. Method and Dirty, they could ride the beat like a cowboy on a wild bull. Whereas U-God, he loved his music to be marching—like *oom-pah*. Ghost, he's real emotional, so a lot of Ghost beats have a chord change or two in them. They're not a one-bar thing, they're a two- or four-bar phrase—they develop inside the beat, like a little story. And they're more soul-oriented, like in a Stax-Volt kind of vein.

Rae, he was a slang master and all he had to have was those drums. If he has a hot pair of drums, he's going to rip it. But it's funny with Rae, because he also has the best voice to go over R&B. If he had been Puffy's MC, he probably would have achieved more mainstream recognition, beause he had that kind of voice, where he could rap over an R&B loop forever. He just sounds good on it, but he's a slang street master so he'll thug it up more.

Inspectah Deck—he's my first bullet in the chamber. If I'm about to attack, I'm sending Inspectah Deck in first. Because you're not going to get past his wit, lyrics, approach, style, and aggression. He'll fuck

I don't give a fuck if you don't know what I'm talking about—this is art. When you go see a painting on the wall and it looks bugged out because you don't know what the fuck he thinking, because he ain't got no benches, no trees there, it's just a splash. The nigga that did it know what the fuck it is.

you up. He's also mad versatile. Method Man is known for his versatility, but Deck is the unsung hero of the Clan in that any beat you put on, he can attack it and rip it.

Method Man and ODB are the most melodic MCs. ODB, you can't tell where his rapping stops and his singing begins. And Method Man to me is the father of that Nelly-style rapping-singing street thing. You listen to that Meth song "Stimulation," where he sings, "I got thirty-six styles on my mind, on my mind . . . " He's the first one on that tip. But he's one of those MCs where if someone bites him, he'll leave it alone. He'll move on.

One other thing I did was I would always put certain sound effects—like husk or static—on to certain voices. In my studio, each Wu-Tang MC had their own compressor set to a certain setting. I had nine compressors, each on a setting. So whoever came over, they could just grab a mic and rip it.

That's why on the earlier music of Wu-Tang, everybody sounds like themselves—they're more recognizable. Once they started making their own solo albums, their voices started changing because their engineers didn't use the same technology I did.

A lot of times you hear people talk about the sound of early Wu-Tang joints—they call them "minimalist." It's true, they *were* minimalist, there was an aesthetic there, no doubt. But at the time, the sound was a product of what I was trying to do as a producer. It was a way to set off MCs.

In early hip-hop a lot of the beats were made by a producer with his idea of what a beat is, not an MC's idea. So musically it might sound good, but it doesn't inspire that feeling in an MC, that spark that makes him want to grab a mic and rip it. I felt that, when you're producing hip-hop, you want the vocals to *be* the instrument. Get out of the way.

I wanted the voices to pull you in as a listener. But I was also producing for MCs, so first and foremost I wanted you to feel our aggression and the texture of our lyrics. If you take a piece like "Chessboxin'," it's spare and basic. In a way, it's nothing *but* rapping. All you can do is jump and go crazy to it. Other producers may have thought about club hits, radio, selling records. The only thing I thought about was MCs sounding aggressive. Forget about the dancing or partying. All you can do is either rap to that shit, or fight to it.

THE DEADLY ART OF RHYME

The backbone of surprise is fusing speed with secrecy.

—CARL VON CLAUSEWITZ

Ghostface Killah's lyrics

There was an old martial arts film that ODB and I used to love. Its more recent title is *Life on the Line,* but the true title from back in the day is *The 60-Second Assassin.* The character's name in the movie is Minute Funk, and around 1983, that was my trade name. My idea was to beat any MC in sixty seconds. And that became the basic Wu-Tang approach, to slice a person's head off quick, like a samurai. Not sitting there going line, line, line, line—all these long lines and you ain't saying nothing. Just—*swissssh.* And he's gone.

I can give you a better explanation of what I mean with a lyric: "I'll defeat your rhyme in just four lines/yes, I'll wax you and tax you and plus save time." I think I first wrote that around '85 or '86, and GZA used to use it in battle. The whole idea was to defeat a motherfucker in four lines. That kind of explosive, straight-out-the-box style became a trademark of the Wu-Tang Clan.

When Wu-Tang came out, we had one big advantage: surprise. At the time, no one was checking for a group like us because the rap game wasn't where it was supposed to be. There was no reality, no imagination. The Afrocentric age was mostly a fad because people weren't really living it—it was more like a look, with the beads and colors. The beats were corny because most producers couldn't rap. Scratching was obsolete, except for Premier. Rawness was out of it. The highest-selling rap at the time was shit like Hammer and Young MC.

So most niggas didn't even recognize the Wu-Tang styles and slang when we hit. I mean, you had never heard a style like Method Man's, and he had six or seven different styles to choose from. MCs like Meth and ODB, they showed niggas a whole new way to make records. Busta Rhymes told me once that after hearing the ODB album, he knew how to make an album. After we sold the formula, people's minds got open. So the style we had was fatal, because it was dangerous and unknown.

There are many ways you could get fucked up in rhyme battle. I could come in scientifically, Gravediggas style, on some verbose, arcane shit you can't even keep up with. Meth could come in goofy singsong on some "Hey-hey, like Fat Albert" and crack you up. Or GZA could come in with the best lyrics you could possibly imagine. That's what he did in "Clan in da Front." There you have lines like, "I'm at the mound/And it's a no hitter/My DJ is the catcher/He's the man/In a way he devise the plan/He hook up the beats with clout/I throw the rhyme into the plate and I strike him out."

One classic example of straight-out-the-box devastation is Deck's first verse in "Triumph." After I heard that, I didn't even want to get on that song. That's how it touched me. You don't really have MCs rhyming like that. He has two lines heavy enough to be four, five, six lines. "Battle-scarred shogun, explosion when my pen hits." Artists ain't writin' like that. "Tremendous ultra violet light blinds forensics." You need to go searchin' to find somebody that's sayin' something so visual, that's just describing stuff like that.

Or "Black Wu jackets queen bees ease the guns in." He's saying that the women brought the guns in the place, but it's so slick you can't even touch it. The average MC woulda been, 'We all rolled to the club, I passed the gun to my shorty.' But that ain't Wu-Tang. "Black Wu jackets queen bees eased the guns in/Rumble with patrolmen, tear gas laced the function."

You hear artists running around talking about jewelry all the time. They wear diamonds, you got ice—which Rae and them mostly started—everybody's wrists is "frosty" and "frozen" and "the bling-bling will blind you"—all these metaphors for jewelry. But who have you ever heard call jewelry actually what it is? It's a mineral, a precious mineral of earth, a stack of crystalline carbon. That's what gives it the shine. It has a history, it's not just a necklace. It could be a woman you had, your wife or your daughter.

But very few MCs use the language on that level. If I'm about, "Yeah I paid 100 thou, and it's bling-bling, and it'll blind you, and when I wear it on my neck, it's so heavy that I walk like this . . ."—then, really, who gives a shit? You want to take it to the next level—to all the levels. Talking about the history of the diamond, where it comes from, what it's about, why it's a precious gem—that's the lyrical side of it.

When I rap about "my pyroclastic flow," I'm talking about my rhyme flow, but the phrase comes from a volcanic eruption. Pyroclastic flow is the lava, heat, ash, and molten rock of a volcano. It goes just *pffffff*—and crushes everything in sight. It flows and turns everything in its path to ashes because it's so hot, so powerful and strong. Or you know, on "Amplified Sample," I say, "I came in, accompanied by deadly rain and wind." That's what I'm talking about: battling with metaphor. I mean, you're comin with two hundred people? Well, I'm coming with actual rain and wind. It's a whole lot more powerful. Who are you gonna be more intrigued by?

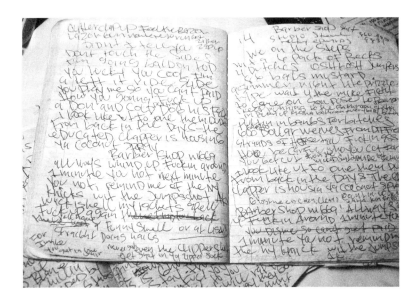

Metaphors like that weren't being used too much back then. And Raekwon had the most abstract slang you could think of: "Champion gear that I rock/You get your boots knocked/They'll attack you like a pit/and lock shit down"—as well as dropping that real street truth, truth so real you could feel it. You hear that in lines like "I be working on the crime side/the *New York Times* side . . . ." You combine those styles and you're invincible.

We get paid from it, it's about selling records, but it's also an art form. It's about being genuine with it and being yourself—just bringing out the creativeness, not doing the same thing everybody else is doing, regardless of whether it don't break through or pop off immediately.

It's like, reach one, teach one. But for me, it's also about the respect level. It's not just how many people are feelin' you, it's *who* is feeling you. In my case, ain't no dumb people running up to me sayin' "Yo, yo, whatchu thinking about when you wrote this . . . ?"' That's how it should be.

U-GOD ON THE SPONTANEOUS JUMP-OFF

Certain people in the group got that rap style that I call the spontaneous jump-off. It's like being able to stand at the foul line and, without backing up and running at the net, just dunk it—BOOM. Just dunk it from standing at the foul line. Not too many people got that type of style, and a bunch of 'em are in Wu-Tang. Certain songs we just know to jump off—spontaneous, atomically. The first two lines get you.

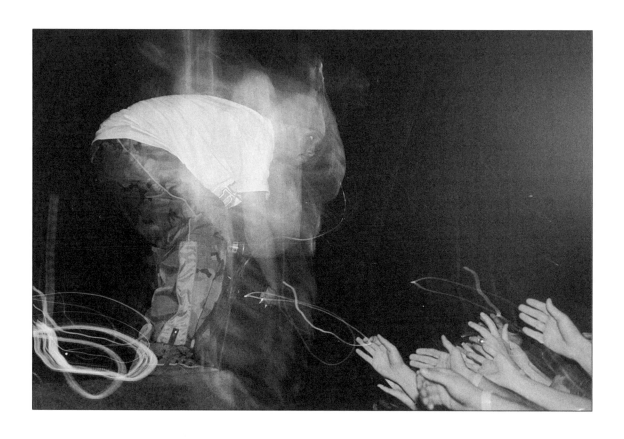

WU-TANG
LIVE

The attraction of the virtuoso for the public is very like that of the circus for the crowd. There is always the hope that something dangerous will happen.

—CLAUDE DEBUSSY

L ive performance has always been a key part of hip-hop. Even if you take it back to the four elements—breaking, graffiti writing, DJing, and rapping—most of it's about a live, spontaneous vibe, just kicking it out in the streets. It makes sense that people consider live performance crucial. But live hip-hop is some crazy shit.

All members of the Wu-Tang came up performing live, that's what we always did: hit the stage, rock the crowd, and break out. But the thing is, we also hit a lot of people on the way to the stage, and they hit us too. That's just how it was. The shows always had violence.

Since Wu-Tang were natural hip-hop niggas, we didn't really rehearse too much. In the beginning, when it was a dictatorship I was running, I set up rehearsals. We'd rehearse in Staten Island, in two different studios that were used by different rock bands. One near Stapleton Projects and the other off of Richmond Terrace near Mariner's Harbor. It was the usual rock practice room: carpet on the floor, soundproof on the walls, some mics, a DAT. As we got more popular we rehearsed at S.I.R. in Manhattan.

But really, after the first two years, we didn't rehearse at all. With Wu-Tang it was just nine niggas spitting rhymes—you don't work on choreography. When you're rocking hip-hop, you're just rocking. The old hip-hop performers, they just throw down. You might be in a club and you never know if you're going to be called to the mic. We played the Garden one day—for an AIDS benefit with Run/DMC—and made up the set list five minutes before going onstage. When we did the Rage Against the Machine Tour, it was spontaneous. We look at the crowd, and come up with ideas, and hit it.

In a way, running a live hip-hop show is like DJing a party. In fact, before every show, our DJ comes up to me and asks, "What do you want to do?" And I look at the crowd and say, "You know what, let's set 'em up like this"—you know, DJ style. And then if some things work, we repeat them.

When we first formed, we started getting a little money from shows. A *little* money. We still were broke and splitting two hundred dollars down to twenty dollars apiece. And then if, say, Dirty needed money for his Pampers, somebody gave a twenty to him. It was rough, but it got better fast. As we were recording the first album, we starting getting gigs for the whole crew just to do the single "Protect Ya Neck." So niggas were going home with eight hundred dollars.

That felt good—you didn't have to shoot nobody. Though there was definitely violence at the shows. It was just part of it.

If you check Wu-Tang's history, you see that even though we did live shows, we never really toured hard. We'd go out for a month or two out of three years. We were always more of a recording group, like the Beatles. But you have to go touch the people. And we like to make it count. I think that with us, when we touched the people they knew they'd been *touched*.

In Philadelphia, I was at a theater showing that hip-hop concert movie *The Show*. The only people the audience gave love to were Biggie, Run/DMC, and Snoop. But even then, if anyone was onstage over twenty minutes, the crowd was yelling "Wu-Tang." If Wu-Tang is on the bill—trust me, you're gonna see some shit. The crowd doesn't know what they're in for.

I've been asked a lot what the wildest gig we ever did was and that's too hard for me to say. But one strong contender is a New Year's show at the Culture Club. That, or the Beacon Theater—the one Ghost describes in a rap. That show was Wu-Tang and Biggie Smalls, the first show we did together. Ghost and Rae had a problem with a *Source* coming out with Biggie on the cover being called "King of New York." They thought *they* were kings of New York. Luckily, they never got a chance to cross paths that night.

But I still say it doesn't get any wilder than the Culture Club. Wild for everybody there—the show, the club, the artists, the fans. Fights breaking out in the middle of the club, guns drawn, two feet away you see one nigga pointing a gun at another nigga, then getting crashed with a chair. And this is all before we even hit the stage.

I remember one kid was disrespecting one of us and I think this was one of my nights. I think I was the one that was amped up that night about this kid showing no kind of respect. Then even after the fight was over, niggas tore the whole place up out of spite. Broke all the windows, busted the whole bar down. *Then* we went to the stage and rocked the mic.

We went through the crowd—split that crowd like Moses splitting the Red Sea. Ripped it. Then this nigga pulls out onstage, and starts *shooting* onstage—and by "this nigga," I mean ODB. ODB pulled out a gun and started firing, hitting the ceiling. Then we jumped into the crowd and broke out. That was a show.

Always make the audience suffer as much as possible.

—ALFRED HITCHCOCK

Most Wu-Tang shows had at least two or three fights in them. In fact, we had enough of a rep for fighting at our own shows that we eventually got banned from New York. I don't mean just New York venues wouldn't book the Wu-Tang Clan. I mean we, as a group and as individuals, weren't even allowed in these New York nightclubs. They basically banned the whole of Staten Island. We just weren't tamed yet. Most of the clubs were owned by the same people. They only started letting us back in about two years ago.

> One of my chief regrets during my years in the theater was that I couldn't sit in the audience and watch me.
>
> —JOHN BARRYMORE

The bad part came when we hit the really big auditoriums, like on the Rage Against the Machine Tour. It wasn't just the places. It was where we were at as a group. When Wu-Tang Clan pulled out of the Rage tour, it broke my heart, but it was done as a democracy. I let everybody do what they wanted to do. I told everybody that this was a very important tour for our careers. I said, "We do this tour right, we can embed ourselves deeply into American culture."

I kept saying, "Let's spread our message to the world." But not everybody was understanding that. When they started backing out, it really hurt me, so I backed out too. I regret it, but I can understand how they felt. Sometimes that hood shit just keeps you in a certain mind frame, and it feels wrong to break out of it. The Wu-Tang has always been a volatile substance and you can't always make it do your bidding. But before we pulled out, those crowds did get rocked.

Now everybody's grown. It's good, there's more respect, more love on the stage. And we know how to rock the crowd better. At our ten-year anniversary show in California, we hadn't seen each other for a long time. There was no rehearsal. We just hit the stage. Afterward, there were all these reviews saying how much we must have rehearsed. It was spontaneous combustion. We get better at knowing when to fall back and when to step up—how to give each other space to shine. It was never conscious, just something we learned over many years.

Even now, the shows still get pretty bananas. It's still nine niggas out there rocking and when we get into our sync—it may be the third or fourth song, when niggas are feeling crazy, and everybody's just like, "Fuck it." That's when it gets pretty crazy out there. That much hasn't really changed since we started.

THE WAY OF THE ABBOT

To lead the people, walk behind them.

—LAO TZU

I am often referred to as the Abbot of Wu-Tang. We originally got the name from kung-fu movies—the abbot is the head of the temple, the one who teaches the monks the styles and philosophies of martial arts. But the word comes up throughout history. In Aramaic, the word *abba* means "father," and variations on it usually refer to a teacher of some kind. The abbot is someone who can advise you and teach you, someone who has experienced things and can explain them to you.

But you can't get that way without being a good student, too. And that's what I think I am. I'm a student *and* a teacher.

I think being the Abbot is something I was born into. Even in my own family, I'm the fourth child and the third son, which together equals seven. That's the God number, the source of light. Dirty broke that down a long time ago. He said that me and him, we're both the third son and the fourth child in our families. We're both the seven in the center. It's like the sun that planets revolve around someone who's in the middle, observing, pulling energy in and sending it out. I really think I've been like that all my life.

As a kid, I was known for being able to analyze things. I was logical. That was one of my first titles, actually—in high school, they called me Mr. Logic. And I became kind of like a judge in the hood.

People came to me to settle area disputes. I settled relationship fights, neighborhood wars. If someone from Park Hill went into Stapleton and shot somebody, the first nigga who got shot would go to my house for bandages. But if that same guy came by the next weekend, he might see the guy that shot him sitting on the couch right here. Because I was involved with everyone. I was in the middle.

What RZA brought together let no man tear asunder.

—METHOD MAN

Even before Wu-Tang was officially a group, I was the nucleus, because I'm the common denominator. Before they knew each other they all knew me. Once we came together, I became the seven in the center of Wu-Tang. It was just my role—to be the source of energy for the rest of the band, the gravitational center that pulls everyone together.

People ask me how I can get all these different MCs—each one being so brilliant and unpredictable—to listen to me. It's hard for me to define how it works, but it goes back a long way.

The common thread was Mathematics. There's always one among you who's the best knower. Within the Wu-Tang Clan, that was me. I had the answers to the most questions at the time. And the truth is magnetic. It attracts everything to it. And that's what I was dealing with—with a true vision and a true past, and my own honesty, the way I dealt with equality.

At the time, some brothers were still stuck out in the street, not living morally. I was already coming to an understanding of myself, but I also understood what they were going through. So I was able to deal with this equilibrium.

At the same time, I knew what I was doing, and I was very firm about it. I wasn't a pushover. I was more like, "This is where it is, this is how it is, and that's that." Brothers respected that. And they respected my judgment.

Back then, Masta Killa was a student of GZA. I was also GZA's student, but even the GZA submitted his enlightenment over to me—as we say, he came over to my guidance. So right there, that gave Masta Killa the freedom to feel the same way.

At that time, my word alone was enough to strike terror. Not because of what I was going to *do* to someone, in a street way, but because the truth is terrifying. I was 100 percent true. I had a true vision, true execution. I never crossed anybody. I'd been true with all these particular people since I was a child. I mean, I'd crossed other people, but with these guys I was always straight and clean. I'd developed this reputation before it ever came down to music.

> If your actions inspire others to dream more, learn more, do more, and become more, you are a leader.
>
> —JOHN QUINCY ADAMS

Of course, there's another side to it, too. Even if you're living righteous and providing a powerful example to others, it helps to have some game if you want niggas to follow you.

MASTA KILLA
ON THE ABBOT

RZA is one of the most beautiful brothers that I know. I learned so much from that brother, what he has given to the world and what he has created as far as a vision. A brother like him, you only gonna see once every twenty-five thousand years.

Back then, Ghost and I were the two top game niggas you could meet. We used to eat for free, drink for free, smoke for free, get everything free—because we could talk our way into anything. That helped us in the business, too. We were able to be like, "Yo, I'm gonna talk you out your watch." And that was crucial to the growth of the Wu-Tang Clan. You have to work the people. You have to get the people in the industry working for *you*.

In times of change, learners inherit the Earth, while the learned find themselves beautifully equipped to deal with a world that no longer exists.

—ERIC HOFFER

THE ABBOT'S RULE OF FOUR

One thing I learned is that with a team like this—with nine generals, nine ninjas, nine strong brothers—the cut-off number is four. It's not a majority, but it doesn't matter. If you got four niggas in your crew that are against something, then it's serious. It's real. Then you have to regroup and consider changing direction.

The cut-off number is four. If I've got four against something, then it's serious. It's real.

Post-Democracy —
Wu-Tang After
Wu-Tang Forever

The crucial turning point for Wu-Tang was in the making of the album *Wu-Tang Forever*. It was 1997—97 being a very serious number in Mathematics—and the term limit of my five-year plan was up. I was open to converting Wu-Tang from the dictatorship it had been to a democracy. What we got was a double album and, around that time, a lot of chaos.

After that, it didn't go back to being a dictatorship, but I slowly tried to resume more control. It wasn't a dictatorship exactly, but some different kind of monarchy. When it was time to do *The W* and *Iron Flag*, I took a lot more control. It was subtle at first, but I think all the Wu-Tang niggas were with it. It was more balanced: it wasn't a total dictatorship, it wasn't a total democracy.

> As we look ahead into the next century, leaders will be those who empower others.
>
> —BILL GATES

Now, in the beginning of this new century, this new millennium, I'm still here to be the Abbot to anyone that's ready and worthy and needs me. I know I have the knowledge and the power to share and I'll do it on the right occasion. But I'm not going to force myself on anyone. With Wu-Tang, I just make myself available, and if my soldiers want me, I'm here.

Many are called, few are chosen, and those niggas in Wu-Tang, they were chosen a long time ago. They're part of me and always will be. And I'll share what knowledge I have with them at any point. What they do will always reflect back on me, whether they know it or not. At least, that's how I look at it.

WUMAN RESOURCES

It was a clique of people. Who all believed in one thing. Gettin' high. And playin'.

—CHARLES MINGUS

Back in the day, brothers like Duke Ellington and Charles Mingus had that same basic approach to making music as I do. Even though they were both ill instrumentalists on their own, they felt that their orchestra—these same few niggas they always worked with—was their real instrument.

But to make that work, you have to accept a certain amount of chaos. That to me was a main principle of Wu-Tang: organized chaos.

The universe is chaotic, yet it does follow a mathematical plan. So it only seems like chaos until you figure out the equation. I knew Wu-Tang was definitely chaotic according to everybody else, but to me it was organized. At least I knew the direction it was going. It's like water. Water is chaotic really, but if you cut a path for it, it will flow.

JOHN GOODMANSON,
AUDIO ENGINEER FOR
IRON FLAG, ON
CHANGING IT UP

They really do everything super ghetto loop style. And then the other thing that was crazy was RZA would change around the order of the verses. We'd have gotten the whole mix together and then he comes in and says, "No, put Ghostface here"—you know, totally change it up. He heard the voices in a very specific way.

In a way, the idea of making "Protect Ya Neck" a group joint was nuts. That's a lot of MCs to sell to listeners in a short amount of time. But in hip-hop, some of the best records made you think of a symphony. A Tribe Called Quest's "The Scenario," Poison Clan's "Crash Two"—you sang those all day. So to have these eight new niggas go out all at once? I knew it would come off.

But even then, it was always about setting up the MCs to fly out on their own. Even the B-side to "Protect Ya Neck" was "Method Man." We were already setting him up to be the first breakout solo artist. It was a way to bring the group further. It was all a conscious decision from the beginning.

BATTLE MANAGEMENT

In the old days, I was producing almost every beat in an MC context because everybody wanted to do a verse to prove how good they were. Even though Wu-Tang was a collective force, there was still an MC competition within it. And with an MC competition, even though everybody's down with each other, everybody still thinks that they're the best. It's like a sibling rivalry. You can't tell one MC he's not better than another on the mic. He won't believe you. You just can't tell a rapper that he's not the best rapper. It's like every boxer thinks he has a chance to be the champion.

So in the old days, when I had a new beat ready, everybody wanted to get on. And that's where the Abbot force came in. Everybody will get a *chance* to get on it, but everybody won't remain on it at the end. I'd screen a lot of verses in the old days and more often than not I'd kick a person off the track.

CAREER MANAGEMENT

Even when we were doing the solo deals, I'd kind of force certain people to certain labels. For example, ODB wanted to go to Def Jam at the beginning, and I'd have to say "We don't need two artists on Def Jam. We have to spread out." So he went to Elektra. He didn't want to go to Elektra, but it was the best thing for the family. We almost had a fistfight over it. The whole clan was there. And that was another thing that showed the Abbot's strength, because he realized, "Wow. He's very serious about what he's trying to do here." And that brought another level of respect.

I wasn't randomly pushing people around. I had to think of everybody because I knew that everybody wasn't thinking about each other.

Once everybody had become a character and developed that character and had fans that recognized the character—after they became popular, basically—it was different. You can imagine how many of us come across some fan in the crowd saying, "Yo, *you* the *best* one!" That happens to all of us! So I think once everybody got to that comfortable position that they were good—and they *were* good—then it wasn't all about screening the verses anymore.

We got to a level of acceptance. We'd accept what this guy did because that's *him* now. He's identified as that. So if Method Man got on the track, whether it was his best or not, he's now identifed as Method Man—so of course it's good. It became good in a more marketable way.

That changed Wu, because it wasn't necessarily about the skills anymore. We accepted the roles we were playing. The first time that started happening was about 1997—around *Wu-Tang Forever*. A few guys had successful solo albums and they were very strong with what they wanted. Other members were satisfied with their position.

It isn't good and it isn't bad. It's a natural evolution. Everybody flowed within it.

THE WORLD
ACCORDING TO RZA

In 2003, I made the album *The World According to RZA*. Initially, the MCs were chosen by different people from different companies helping me out. I sent my music out to them, and as far as the choices of artists, it was done very A&R-like. It wasn't done spiritually.

But once I met the people who I was dealing with, that's when the spirituality came in. Because some people didn't make the album, but maybe their friends made it, or someone from their community made it. But whoever made it got on because of their spirit or how they connected with me. In the end, it was a very organic process. Some people came in with egos, and when I was doing this album, it was like doing the first Wu-Tang album—I wasn't accepting no egos. I was accepting only submission to what I was trying to do.

The experience was a flashback, in a way. By this time I'd sold millions of records, become so-called "world famous." And in my opin-

ion, the hunger of hip-hop in America had decreased. There was so much money involved with it. When I came to do this record in Europe, I saw the hunger of 1992 in these MCs. Almost every person on that album came in with the hunger. They came in—no money, no nothing—just to rock.

To get some people in the studio in America you might have to put up a hundred grand. And what happened to me on a producing level, it made me remember: This is about hip-hop. It's about just making your music and *going,* just creating and creating, nonstop, no sleep, just going. It was a resurrection in a way. Sometimes you've got to travel halfway around the world to get reborn.

WU-TANG
THE SAGA CONTINUES

My vision of the Wu-Tang mission is never going to change. What I'm striving for now is the same as what I've been striving for since I started—I'm striving for all the twelve jewels of life.

As they teach in Mathematics, all men should seek the twelve jewels of life: knowledge, wisdom, understanding, freedom, justice, equality, food, clothing, shelter, love, peace, and happiness.

A man must first obtain knowledge. And knowledge will lead him to wisdom—his ways, actions, and the way he speaks. A man who knows how to speak can bring forth understanding. And when a man gains understanding, he understands whether or not he's free. Once you're mentally free you're going to automatically know how to be physically free. But freedom operates under a law of justice. You may be free to smack somebody in the face, but then the law of justice will apply, meaning they can smack you back. Justice is a self-balancing scale that makes all men deal with one another with equality.

So then you can live as a man—whether you're doing business or farming—you can step into this world, look for your food, clothing, and shelter. And the only thing to achieve after that is love, peace, and happiness. Once you have love, you're going to look for peace. What's love without peace? If you love somebody and they don't love you? Then what you get is war. People spread love without peace, or peace without love—what results is always a form of war. Happiness is complete satisfaction with yourself. If you have to keep looking outside yourself for happiness you'll never find it.

So my first goal is to achieve all those jewels for myself. And what I want for myself I want for my brothers—the Clan. And then, I want it for all mankind. That's been my mission from day one—it just keeps evolving to the next step.

I think that there are a lot of things that will be shared by Wu-Tang. Some of us are ahead and some of us are behind, but as they say in the Bible, "The first shall be last and the last shall be first." In our case, that means that the ones that you thought the least of may become the greatest of us. And the ones you thought the most of, they may become the least.

> Every child is an artist. The problem is how to remain an artist once he grows up.
>
> —PICASSO

Keeping the attitude of a child is very, very important in life. I try to keep that in me every day. The child you were is what makes you the man you are, and you always have to reflect back. Even if a child cries, five minutes later he's back jumping around again. So to have a child's heart is gold. It's the fountain of youth. There's no way to slow your life down, there's no way to regain youth except through your own feeling. It's what's inside your heart.

The funny thing is, hip-hop itself is a family, and every next generation is the children. Today, this family goes across the whole globe. I think I always knew hip-hop would be a worldwide phenomenom. I knew it from the brothers from the Old School—and that what they had, and what it would be in the future, had a lot to do with what Wu-Tang would do next.

I knew that GZA and myself were the babies of the Old School guys—from Force MDs, to Cold Crush Brothers, to the Furious Five, Grandmaster Flash, the Fantastic Five, the Disco Four Plus One More, the Funky Four Plus One More. At the time we were coming up, the New School brothers were Rakim, KRS-One, Big Daddy Kane, Biz Markie, Marley Marl, the whole Juice Crew team, as well as brothers like Just Ice and other MCs that didn't make it. We were absorbing all of it back then, we were the ones being nurtured by them. Who knows who's being nurtured now?

There's always another hidden chamber waiting for you to discover it. Hip-hop is a chamber in itself and right now it's the leading force of the world. It's like rock was in the '60s and soul and funk were in the '70s. But there's always another chamber that's waiting for another generation to come along and unlock it.

Wu-Tang's always going to have something to share. It may come from our children—and we have a lot. Or it may come from our listeners. It may come from a disciple of a chamber, the people that were influenced by the mentality of it. Sometimes the listeners understand more than the speaker. Sometimes the speaker is more like a radio—

he's just transmitting the message. Sometimes that listener is the one that's *really* going to get sparked.

In a way, that's the whole point of the thirty-sixth chamber. That's the chamber in which you share the knowledge with the world. Some say you should never teach the arts and styles of the Wu-Tang. But we've put them out into the world. For those who seek knowledge, it's there. But you have to seek it out, do the knowledge, and understand it on your own.

Grateful acknowledgment is made to the following for the right to reprint lyrics from the following songs:

"Protect Ya Neck" by Gary Grice, Clifford Smith, Corey Woods, Dennis Coles, Jason Hunter, Lamont Hawkins, Russell Jones, and Robert Diggs © 1993 Careers-BMG Music Publishing, Inc. (BMI)/Wu-Tang Publishing (BMI)/Ramecca Publishing (BMI)/BMG Songs, Inc. (ASCAP). All rights for the US obo Wu-Tang Publishing (BMI) and Ramecca Publishing (BMI) administered by Careers-BMG Music Publishing, Inc. (BMI).

"Bring Da Ruckus" by Gary Grice, Clifford Smith, Corey Woods, Dennis Coles, Jason Hunter, Lamont Hawkins, Russell Jones, Robert Diggs © 1993 Careers-BMG Music Publishing, Inc. (BMI)/Wu-Tang Publishing (BMI)/BMG Songs, Inc. (ASCAP). All rights for the US obo Wu-Tang Publishing (BMI) administered by Careers-BMG Music Publishing, Inc. (BMI).

"C.R.E.A.M." by Gary Grice, Clifford Smith, Corey Woods, Dennis Coles, Jason Hunter, Lamont Hawkins, Russell, Jones, Robert Diggs, Isaac Hayes, and David Porter © 1993 Careers-BMG Music Publishing, Inc. (BMI)/Wu-Tang Publishing (BMI)/BMG Sons, Inc. (ASCAP)/Irving Music Inc. (BMI). All rights for the US obo Wu-Tang Publishing (BMI) administered by Careers-BMG Publishing, Inc. (BMI)

"Triumph" by Gary Grice, Clifford Smith, Corey Woods, Dennis Coles, Jason Hunter, Lamont Hawkins, Russell Jones, Robert Diggs, and Elgin Turner © 1997 Careers-BMG Music Publishing, Inc. (BMI)/Wu-Tang Publishing (BMI)/Ramecca Publishing (BMI)/BMG Songs, Inc.

image credits

Map on page ix by Mark Stein

Illustrations on pages 40, 41, 43, 50, 51, 52, 67, 101, 102, 110, 111, and 112 by Ben Gibson

Photographs on pages 3, 7, 15, 19, 23, 27, 31, 35, and 90 © Michael Lavine

Photographs on pages 11, 53, 54, 55, 56, 64, 66 and 111 © Sophia Chang

Photographs on pages 38, 80, 81, 92, 94, 95, 97, 99, and 106 © Frank 151 Media Group, LLC. **F**
276 Canal Street, 7 West,
New York, NY 10013

Photographs on pages 122, 126, 137, 144, 149, 154, 161, 167, 172, 177, 182, 210, 213, 214, 217, 218, 221 and 222 © Craig Wetherby

Wu-Tang logos on pages 41 and 63 © Mathematics

Comic strip on page 84 © Gibralter Entertainment LLC

Photograph of Emulator SP-1200 on page 196 courtesy of E-MU. Special thanks to Ed Rudnick.

Photographs of the Ensoniq EPS, Ensoniq EPS-16 Plus, ASR-10 on pages 196 and 197 courtesy of Route 66 Studios. Special thanks to Richard Walsh.

The saga continues . . .